Rachael Ray

30-Minute Meals

30-Minute Meals

LAKE ISLE PRESS   NEW YORK

All inquiries should be addressed to:

Lake Isle Press, Inc.

16 West 32nd Street

Suite 10-B

New York, NY 10001

lakeisle@earthlink.net

Library of Congress Catalog Card Number: 98-75278
ISBN: 1-891105-03-5

Book design by Ellen Swandiak

Photography by Colleen Brescia

25 24 23 22 21 20

Dedicated to my mom, Elsie Providenzia

You taught me that living the good life is as simple as eating good food ... and that peace is found in the smiles of our loved ones (so stay close to home)

acknowledgments

Special thanks to all the wonderful cooks in my family:
Grampa Emmanuel Nini, Brother Emmanuel, Sister Maria Diano,
Gramma Betar, Nanny Moore, and James Claude (my pop).

Thanks to Dan DiNicola. You are as wonderful to know as you are
to work with.

Thanks to all of the wonderful, giving friends and fans of the
30-Minute Meal. Thanks for your supportive letters and all the
thoughtful gifts — I love the homemade potholders, the herb
plants, the homegrown garlic, the blue potatoes, and most of all,
the kind thoughts each of you have shared with me. I know how
grateful Dan is for the mail he receives as well.

Thanks to all of those who have helped make the *30-Minute Meal*
possible: everyone at WRGB, World's First Television Station,
with special thanks to Joe Coscia. Thanks to the gang at
P.C./Golub Corporation for inviting and encouraging me to teach
my kind of cooking, my way.

Thanks to all my friends who, over the years, have shared their
love of food and fun — those who have saved seats for me at
their tables, and room for me in their hearts, thank you.

Thanks to Hiroko Kiiffner and the fine team of artists and editors
who made this cookbook way-cool.

Thanks to God for my wonderful life. Nice job, Big Guy.

Thanks to my dog Boo, who had to eat a lot of my mistakes.

contents

quick-reference

TOP 10 MEALS

Recipes Vox Populi: These meals got the most requests for recipes after airing as *The 30-Minute Meal* segment, a weekly feature on WRGB news.

TOP 10 MEALS WITH FEWER THAN 10 INGREDIENTS

TOP 10 KIDS' FAVORITES

Most Requested by the Munchkin Jet Set

contents

30-minute pastas

Cupboard Cooking ... Pastas from the Kitchen Cabinet

Restaurant Row ... Pastas from the Menu of your Favorite Italian Restaurant

Pastabilities ... More Pasta Meals in Minutes

Presto Pestos

Gran'pa Emmanuel's Pasta Concoctions

salads and other green stuff

Three Too Simple Dressings for Green Salads

Bistro Salads

Salads As Suppers

Warm, Leafy Greens

make your own take-out

30-minute comfort foods

Mediterranean Comforts

Tex-Mex One Pots

Continental Favorites

great gatherings

Five Fabulous Meatballs

introduction

The *30-Minute Meal* began as a cooking class offered in the kitchen of a small marketplace and grew into a feature on the local news in the Albany, New York, television market. *The 30-Minute Meal* segments are as much about life as they are about food. There are no chefs in white coats on TV studio kitchen sets, or wealthy housewives in sterilized,  over-applianced super-kitchens. *The 30-Minute Meal* series features someone who looks a lot like you, cooking in a real kitchen that looks a lot like yours, making something that looks really good — something that you know you could do, too.

This book does the same thing — it is about can-do cooking, can-do better living. Anyone can cook. You need not have a kitchen like Martha's to enjoy fine food and a rich life. Cooking can and should make you feel good about yourself. Relax. Fill your belly with some good stuff and have fun doing it.

—Rachael Ray

When I was a boy, my mother and aunt cooked. Great food, wonderful smells. The women cooked; I sat back and ate. Later I learned that men cooked, too. I envied them, I wanted to learn, but it was too late. Too busy, not enough time. Besides, all those high-falutin' cooking shows intimidated me — the perfectionist. Ah well, maybe in the next life.

Then along came Rachael, who showed me how easy it all was — and in less time than it took to order out. Each week for our TV spot, she instructed, I cooked. And it worked. The culmination of these informal lessons and unrehearsed TV get-togethers arrived when I cooked a multicourse meal for my kids when they all came home for vacation. I was as nervous as a kid at his first recital; they, who had never seen me create more than a rock-hard meat loaf, were bemused. Finally, I sat at the head of the table watching my family eat food I had prepared in less time than I had imagined.

Go ahead, ask the kids. They still can't believe it. If this culinary klutz can do it, so can you. Thank you, Rachael, for showing me how easy it is to cook terrific meals.

—Dan DiNicola

3 tips to chew on

"DON'T MEASURE WITH INSTRUMENTS, USE YOUR HANDS. You're not baking or conducting experiments for the government — just feel your way through."

"SMELL AND TASTE THE INGREDIENTS AS YOU GO. Learning about food and flavor is what this book is about. By tasting and sniffing your way through many different types of recipes, your palate will play matchmaker and you will learn how to associate flavors and textures that complement one another."

"COMMIT YOURSELF TO NOT BUYING TAKE-OUT FOOD MORE THAN TWICE THIS WEEK. Cook the other five nights. Get the hang of it. Change the recipes to reflect your own tastes. It is the sincere hope of the author that you will never have to buy another cookbook, including one of her own, ever again. Cooking quick and easy recipes night after night will build you a pantry and the confidence to learn to live on your own recipes for the rest of your life."

HANDFUL

about 3
tablespoons

•

PALMFUL

about 2
tablespoons

•

**HALF
A PALMFUL**

you do the math

•

A PINCH

about 1/4 teaspoon

•

**A FEW GOOD
PINCHES**

about 1 teaspoon

•

**ONCE AROUND
THE PAN**

about 1 tablespoon
of liquid

•

**TWICE AROUND
THE PAN**

more math: about
2 tablespoons,
3 or 4 would be
1/4 cup

glossary

Hang Out
Let it: cook, simmer, stand at room temperature
. . . whatever the previous direction was.

When the Garlic Speaks
Referring to the sizzling sound that garlic makes
in oil as it begins to heat. This is the sound of
the garlic telling you to add more stuff to the pan
now.

To peel garlic, place the cloves on a cutting
board. Lay the blade of your knife flat across the
top of the cloves and give them a good, strong
whack with the heel of your hand. The cloves
should pop out and away from the skin.

Give It Feet
If you are new to the use of kitchen knives, you
are not ready to be slicing up round objects:
onions, potatoes, carrots, tomatoes. Give them
feet first. Split the products down the center and
place them flat side down. To have whole, round
slices, trim away a sliver of one side to make it
lay flat on the board.

equipment

You need:

☐ A big, straight-edged knife — cheap ones are fine, just buy a sharpener, too.

☐ The largest cutting board you can find.

☐ A big pot for boiling pasta.

☐ A big nonstick frying pan for everything else.

☐ A food processor, if you like pesto.

Knives

☐ Whenever you use a knife, shake hands with the handle. Choke-up on the bat — place your hand firmly around the handle, where it joins the blade. NEVER balance your index finger on top of blade — you will cut that fingertip off one day.

☐ Always keep the fingers of the opposite hand curled under.

☐ Firmly grip the food product you are chopping — it is an inanimate object.

☐ The board and the products should be dry. "Slippery When Wet" applies to more than roads.

30-minute
pastas

Cupboard Cooking ... Pastas from the Kitchen Cabinet

Aglio Olio: Garlic and Oil Pasta

Pasta Puttanesca

Linguine with White Clam Sauce

Linguine with Red Clam Sauce

Linguine with Sicilian Tuna Marinara

Restaurant Row ... Pastas from the Menu of your Favorite Italian Restaurant

Spaghetti Carbonara: Pasta with Bacon and Eggs

Penne with Classic Bolognese Meat Sauce

Basilico: Tomato-Basil Sauce

Marinara Sauce

Arrabiata: Spicy Tomato Sauce "In a Hurry"

Pastabilities ... More Pasta Meals in Minutes

Chicken Short-Cut-a-Tore: Fast Classic Cacciatore

Pasta Abruzzese: Penne with Sausage, Fennel, and Tomato Sauce

Pasta Amatriciana: Penne with Pancetta, Tomato, and Crushed Red Pepper Sauce

Pasta with Big-Belly Portobello Sauce

Pasta with Roasted Eggplant Sauce

Roasted Red Pepper Sauce

You Won't Be Single for Long Vodka-Cream Sauce

Mamma Elsa's Pasta with Peas, Prosciutto, and Onion

The Three R's: Rigatoni, Rapini, and Ricotta Salata Pasta

Presto Pestos

Classic Basil Pesto

Parsley Pesto

Sugoloso: Sun-Dried Tomato and Basil Pesto

Spinach-Walnut Pesto

Artichoke Crema Pesto

Sesame-Cilantro Pesto

Gran'pa Emmanuel's Pasta Concoctions

Emmanuel Nini's Ziti with Sausage and Cannellini

Manny's Many-Herb Sauce with Walnuts

Manny's Sweet and Sour Sauce

Sicilian Sausage and Fennel Pasta

I remember concluding at a very young age that if you wanted to be around the laughter, the food, and the fun, you needed to be around the kitchen table. There was always room for an extra chair in case another somebody should just drop by. There was always enough food to go around no matter how many mouths were working up appetites by chewing on their opinions too hard. Between the courses, while the smells from the stovetop worked on your stomach, discussions about life's little lessons or just some good, juicy gossip — of a quiet and kind nature by today's standards — would build up your appetite for conversation and companionship.

The kitchen table is where it's at.

When my mamma was just a girl, her kitchen table would walk itself outside onto the lawn when the size of the kitchen could no longer accommodate the number of Sunday callers who came to fill up on her daddy's food and family fun.

Gran'pa Emmanuel filled his Sunday tables with big pots of pasta and sauce. The pastas that fill the menus of today's gourmet restaurants were to him simple, inexpensive dishes that could be made in great quantities for little or no money. At the end of the table, he would put out his own melons and a three-gallon tub of ice cream. He'd split the melons in half and fill each of the cantaloupe bowls with two scoops of vanilla. After the meal, all the children would follow Emmanuel as if he were the Pied Piper. From the kitchen table he would lead them down by the water, where seats he had carved into old fallen trees were waiting for them. The kids would sit in their wooden thrones and listen to Emmanuel's stories and songs about his life as a little boy growing up on the edge of the Mediterranean Sea.

Food is nostalgia. The smell of good, simple food can take you back to all the good times in your life and make you forget all the bad.

Pasta is an easy, inexpensive, simple supper. Place a big bowl of it in the middle of your kitchen table and see what happens.

CUPBOARD COOKING . . . . Pastas from the Kitchen Cabinet

You can cook all of these dishes out of your cabinet — no joke.

By keeping:

☐ 4 boxes linguine

☐ 1 jar oil-cured black olives

☐ 1 bottle crushed red pepper flakes

☐ 2 cans whole baby clams

☐ 3 cans (28 ounces each) crushed tomatoes

☐ 2 tins flat anchovies

☐ 1 jar capers

☐ 2 cans clam broth or bottles of clam juice

☐ 1 bottle red wine

☐ 1 can (6 ounces) white-meat tuna packed in water

☐ 2 bulbs garlic

You can make:

☐ Pasta Puttanesca

☐ Linguine with White Clam Sauce

☐ Linguine with Red Clam Sauce

☐ Aglio Olio: Garlic and Oil Pasta

☐ Linguine with Sicilian Tuna Marinara

By buying:

☐ Fresh flat-leaf parsley

☐ Fresh thyme

☐ Italian bread

On your way home once a week.

All pasta dishes are for one pound of pasta, feeding up to four. I can eat enough for two, then have a late-night snack and a lunch left over. I suggest making full recipes, even if you're alone. You can never have too many tasty leftovers — plus, leftovers make great neighbors when they're shared with "the guy next door."

Aglio Olio:
Garlic and Oil Pasta

1 pound linguine

5 cloves garlic, minced

1/4 teaspoon crushed red pepper (2 pinches or a couple of shakes)

1/4 to 1/3 cup extra-virgin olive oil (4 or 5 times around the pan)

5 anchovy filets (see Note)

A handful fresh flat-leaf parsley, chopped (Just rip it away from a cleaned bunch.)

Freshly ground black pepper, to taste

Note: Keep the rest of the can in a baggie in the fridge for your next dish. Even if you hate anchovies, you won't taste them in any of these dishes — I swear.

Cook pasta until it's al dente — still slightly firm to the bite. In a large skillet over medium heat, cook garlic and pepper in until it speaks. Add anchovies and stir them in oil with a wooden spoon until they disappear. Toss drained pasta into this pan. Coat the pasta evenly with the garlic and oil and anchovies. Add parsley and black pepper. Toss and taste. Adjust pepper and add a pinch of salt, if you feel it's necessary. Dump into a large oval dish. With greens and bread, feeds four.

Pasta Puttanesca

2 tablespoons (twice around the pan) extra-virgin olive oil

3 cloves garlic, minced

A shake or two of crushed red pepper flakes

4 anchovies

1 can (28 ounces) crushed tomatoes

2 tablespoons (a palmful) capers

A palmful pitted oil-cured black olives

A palmful chopped fresh flat-leaf parsley

1 pound linguine, cooked until al dente

Heat oil, garlic, and crushed red pepper over medium heat in a skillet. When garlic speaks, add anchovies and cook until they melt away. Add tomatoes, capers, olives, and parsley. Add cooked pasta to pan. Heat through. Dump onto serving platter. Serves up to 4.

> "Puttanesca is derived from the Italian word for a lady of the night — this dish is spicy, fast, and easy. Easy to figure out where we got the name."

Linguine with White Clam Sauce

3 cloves garlic, minced

2 pinches crushed red pepper flakes

1/4 cup extra-virgin olive oil (2 or 3 times around the pan)

2 or 3 anchovies (for natural salt and as a flavor enhancer)

3/4 cup clam broth (Half a can — save the rest in a dish, not in the can; keep in fridge after opening.)

2 tablespoons (a palmful) chopped fresh thyme (found in produce section)

A handful fresh flat-leaf parsley, ripped from a bunch and chopped

1 can (14 ounces) whole baby clams, drained

1 pound linguine, cooked until al dente

Freshly ground black pepper, to taste

Heat garlic and crushed red pepper in oil over medium heat until garlic speaks by moving around in oil. Add anchovies. Stir with wooden spoon until they melt away in the olive oil. Bring up heat to medium high. Add broth, thyme, pepper and parsley all at once. Dump in clams. Shake pan to combine sauce. Drop in cooked pasta. Toss pasta in sauce. Turn off heat and let stand for a few minutes, until liquid is absorbed. Dump onto platter and enjoy. Feeds 4.

Linguine with Red Clam Sauce

3 cloves garlic, minced

2 pinches crushed red pepper flakes

1/4 cup extra-virgin olive oil (2 or 3 times around the pan)

2 or 3 anchovies (for natural salt and as a flavor enhancer)

1/2 cup (a couple good shots) red wine

1/2 cup clam broth (A third of a can — save the rest in a dish, not a can, and keep in fridge after opening.)

1 can (14 ounces) whole baby clams, drained

2 tablespoons (a palmful) chopped fresh thyme (found in produce section)

A handful fresh flat-leaf parsley, ripped from a bunch and chopped

1 can (28 ounces) crushed tomatoes

1 pound linguine, cooked until al dente

Freshly ground black pepper, to taste

Heat garlic and crushed red pepper in oil over medium heat until garlic speaks by moving around in oil. Add anchovies. Stir with wooden spoon until they melt away in the olive oil. Bring up heat to medium high. Add wine, broth, clams, thyme, and parsley all at once. Let clams soak up wine for a minute. Add tomatoes. Shake pan to combine sauce. Drop in cooked pasta. Toss pasta in sauce. Dump onto platter and enjoy. Feeds up to 4.

Linguine with Sicilian Tuna Marinara

3 tablespoons (three times around the pan) extra-virgin olive oil

4 cloves garlic, minced

A couple shakes crushed red pepper flakes

1 can (12 ounces) Albacore tuna, packed in water, drained, and broken up with a fork

1 can (28 ounces) crushed tomatoes

A palmful chopped fresh flat-leaf parsley

1 pound linguine, cooked until al dente

In a deep skillet, heat olive oil, garlic, and crushed red pepper over medium heat until garlic speaks. Add tuna meat and sauté until tuna is completely flaked and warm through. When the bottom of the pan is covered with nice fishy mush, add crushed tomatoes and the chopped parsley. Heat through and reduce heat to low until pasta is cooked and drained. Dump cooked linguine into the pan and toss thoroughly with sauce. Turn out onto a serving dish or serve right from the hot pan with crusty bread and a green salad. Feeds 4.

RESTAURANT ROW . . .
Pastas from the Menu of Your Favorite Italian Restaurant

Spaghetti Carbonara: Pasta with Bacon and Eggs

1/4 pound pancetta (see Note), chopped in 1/2-inch pieces

1 pound linguine or spaghetti

3 cloves garlic, minced

3 tablespoons extra-virgin olive oil (3 times around the pan)

2 eggs, beaten with a splash of milk and a couple of tablespoons of the boiling water the pasta cooks in

A couple shakes crushed red pepper flakes (optional)

1/2 cup grated Parmigiano Reggiano or Romano cheese, plus extra for the table

A handful chopped fresh flat-leaf parsley (optional)

Freshly ground black pepper, to taste

> Note: Pancetta is Italian rolled bacon with pepper; it's available at deli counters.

Cook the pancetta in a small pan over medium-high heat. Once it begins to brown, remove from heat and place it on paper towels to absorb the grease. Drop your pasta into boiling salted water and let it cook for 5 minutes before you start the sauce. Cook the pasta until al dente. (Don't forget to take a few spoonfuls of boiling water from the pasta pot and add it to your scrambled egg mixture.)

Heat garlic and olive oil in a big skillet or frying pan over very low heat. Add crushed red pepper flakes if you like extra heat. Dump the pasta into a colander, give it a quick rinse, and drain it well. Turn the heat up on the garlic oil from low to medium. Toss the pasta in the pan with the garlic oil and coat the pasta evenly. Toss in the pancetta pieces. Pour the egg mixture evenly over the pasta. Toss the pasta fast and firmly. Turn the heat off. Add cheese, parsley, and a generous dose of black pepper. Serve it up hot, with extra cheese and pepper on hand. Feeds 4.

Penne with Classic Bolognese Meat Sauce

1 pound ground beef, pork and veal mix (available at the butcher counter), or extra-lean ground beef if you are watching your diet

Cracked black pepper, to taste

4 cloves garlic, minced

1/2 teaspoon (a pinch or two) crushed red pepper flakes

2 pinches allspice (the secret ingredient)

1/2 medium Spanish onion

1 cup canned low-sodium, no-fat beef broth

A couple of glugs red wine (about 1/3 cup, optional but recommended)

1 can (28 ounces) crushed tomatoes

A palmful chopped fresh flat-leaf parsley

1 pound penne or rigatoni pasta

Grated Parmigiano Reggiano cheese

Brown meat, seasoned with a little black pepper, in a deep skillet or frying pan over medium high heat. Add garlic, crushed red pepper and allspice. Grate the onion, using a handheld grater, directly into the pan. Cook another 3 to 5 minutes to soften onion. Add broth and wine. Give the pan a good shake. Scrape up any good bits from the bottom of the pan. Add tomatoes and parsley. Give the pan another good shake. Reduce heat to low and simmer while you cook the pasta. Toss with pasta cooked until al dente. Serve with bread and a green salad and grated cheese for the pasta. Feeds 4.

Basilico: Tomato-Basil Sauce

3 tablespoons extra-virgin olive oil (3 times around the pan)

3 cloves garlic, minced

2 cans (28 ounces each) crushed tomatoes, or diced in juice if you like chunky tomato sauce

20 leaves fresh basil, roughly cut or torn

Heat olive oil and garlic in a deep saucepan over medium heat. When the garlic speaks, add tomatoes and heat through. Stir in basil leaves and reduce heat to low. Simmer until pasta of choice is cooked until al dente. This is enough sauce for up to 1 1/2 pounds pasta.

Marinara Sauce

In addition to the ingredients for Basilico Sauce,
you will need:

3 stems fresh oregano, leaves stripped from stems and chopped

A palmful of fresh flat-leaf parsley

Freshly ground black pepper, to taste

Follow method described in preceding recipe, adding the additional herbs and black pepper when you stir in the basil.

> "To sweeten any tomato sauce, add 1/2 a minced onion with the garlic and let it soften and sweeten over medium-low heat for 10 minutes before adding tomato products."

Arrabiatta: Spicy Tomato Sauce "In a Hurry"

In addition to the ingredients for Basilico sauce,
you will need:

Several shakes crushed red pepper flakes, about 1/2 teaspoon

Follow method described in Basilico Sauce recipe, adding the crushed red pepper with the garlic when first heating the oil.

PASTABILITIES . . .
More Pasta Meals in Minutes

Chicken Short-Cut-a-Tore: Fast, Classic Cacciatore

1 pound penne or rigatoni

2 pieces each boneless, skinless breasts and thighs rubbed with a little balsamic vinegar

3 cloves garlic, minced

A couple of shakes (1/4 teaspoon) crushed red pepper flakes

3 tablespoons extra-virgin olive oil (two or three times around the pan)

3 portobello mushroom tops, each halved, then sliced thin

Coarse salt, to taste

1 can (28 ounces) crushed tomatoes

A handful chopped fresh flat-leaf parsley

Grated Parmigiano Reggiano cheese, for the table

Start a pot of salted water to boil. Cook pasta until al dente — still slightly firm to the bite.

Heat a nonstick griddle or skillet over high heat and a second skillet or deep frying pan over medium heat. Cook the chicken on the nonstick griddle for 5 minutes on each side and turn off heat.

In the other skillet, while chicken is cooking, heat garlic and crushed red pepper in oil until garlic speaks. Add mushrooms, coat with oil, sprinkle with salt, and cover. Check after 5 minutes. A dark gravy of portobello juices should have formed. If the mushroom slices are not dark and soft, give the pan a shake, replace lid, and cook another couple of minutes. Add tomatoes and parsley. Sauce should be a rich reddish brown. Slice chicken on diagonal and drop into sauce. Heat through a minute or two. Add cooked, drained pasta to sauce in the pan. Toss and dump out onto serving platter. Top with grated cheese and serve with tossed green salad. Feeds 4 to 6.

Pasta Abruzzese: Penne with Sausage, Fennel, and Tomato Sauce

1 pound bulk sweet sausage (available at the butcher counter)

1/2 medium Spanish onion, finely chopped or processed with fennel

1 bulb fresh fennel, tops trimmed and first layer of skin pulled away; quarter the bulb, then process or chop into fine dice

3 cloves garlic, minced

1 cup low-sodium chicken broth

1 can (28 ounces) crushed tomatoes

A handful chopped fresh flat-leaf parsley

1 pound penne or rigatoni cooked until al dente (still slightly firm to the bite)

Heat a deep skillet over medium-high heat. Add the sausage, breaking it up and browning the crumbles. Remove sausage to a bowl lined with paper towels and let stand to drain away grease. Return pan to heat.

Add onion, fennel, and garlic. Cook for 5 minutes, giving the pan a shake now and then. Add broth and tomatoes. Heat through. Dump sausage back in and add parsley. Stir while bringing to a boil. When sauce bubbles, drop heat to low and let simmer until pasta is ready to toss with sauce and serve. Feeds up to 6 with good, crusty bread.

Pasta Amatriciana: Penne with Pancetta, Tomato, and Crushed Red Pepper Sauce

1/4 pound pancetta, chopped

2 tablespoons extra-virgin olive oil (twice around the pan)

3 cloves garlic, minced

A couple shakes crushed red pepper flakes

1/2 medium Spanish onion, minced or grated with a hand grater

1 can (28 ounces) crushed tomatoes

2 sprigs fresh oregano, chopped

A palmful chopped fresh flat-leaf parsley

1 pound penne or rigatoni, cooked until al dente

In a big skillet or frying pan, brown pancetta over medium heat. Remove from pan and drain on paper towels. Wipe out pan.

Add olive oil, garlic, and crushed pepper to pan. Heat until garlic speaks. Add onion. Cook 5 minutes to sweeten onion. Add tomatoes and herbs. Stir in reserved pancetta. Heat through and reduce heat to low. Simmer until pasta is cooked, drained, and ready to serve. Combine sauce and pasta in hot pot and dump onto serving platter. Feeds 4 with a green salad.

Pasta with Big-Belly Portobello Sauce

1 pound penne or rigatoni pasta
2 tablespoons (twice around the pan) extra-virgin olive oil
3 cloves garlic, minced
A couple pinches crushed red pepper flakes
4 portobello mushroom tops, thinly sliced
Coarse salt, to taste
1 can (28 ounces) crushed tomatoes
A palmful chopped fresh flat-leaf parsley
Grated Parmigiano Reggiano cheese, for the table

Boil salted water in deep pasta pot. Cook the pasta until al dente, or still slightly firm to the bite. When you drain the pasta, cold-shock it with running water to stop the cooking process and toss it into the same pot as your sauce to combine it thoroughly.

While the pasta is cooking, heat the biggest skillet or frying pan you've got over medium-high heat. Add oil, garlic, and crushed red pepper. As soon as the garlic speaks by beginning to sizzle in the oil, dump in the portobello slices. Coat them with the oil with a good shake or two of the pan. Sprinkle them with a little salt.

Cover the pan with a lid or foil and reduce heat to medium low. Let the mushrooms cook for 10 minutes, or until deep brown and soft. There should be a good amount of mushroom gravy in the bottom of the pan. Add the can of tomatoes and a palmful of chopped parsley. Heat through and give the pan a good shake. The sauce will be a nice reddish brown and will have a beefy taste. Combine with pasta and dump onto a platter. Serve with shaved or grated Parmigiano or Asiago cheese, bread, and a green salad. Feeds up to 4.

I always make a full recipe even for just myself — leftover pasta makes a great late-night snack or light lunch.

Pasta with Roasted Eggplant Sauce

1 medium eggplant, 1 to 1 1/2 pounds

3 tablespoons extra-virgin olive oil (a few good glugs)

2 cloves garlic, popped from skin

A handful chopped fresh flat-leaf parsley

Coarse salt and black pepper, to taste

1 can (28 ounces) crushed tomatoes

1 pound pasta, cooked until al dente (still slightly firm to the bite)

Heat oven to 450° F. Cut several slits in the skin of one side of the eggplant. Place whole eggplant with slit side up directly on an oven rack on the middle shelf. Cook for 15 minutes. While eggplant is roasting, cook pasta. Remove eggplant and let stand on counter for 5 minutes.

Heat olive oil and garlic in a dish in microwave oven on high for 20 seconds or warm in a small saucepan until garlic speaks. Hold the whole cooked eggplant over the top of a food processor or blender. Peel the eggplant like a banana with the use of a paring knife by holding the stem in one hand and sliding the knife under sections of the skin with the other. When you've peeled away the skin, cut the flesh of the eggplant loose from the stem and let it drop into the processor or blender. Dump in the garlic, oil, parsley, and salt and pepper, to taste.

If you stop here, this eggplant puree makes a wonderful dip for vegetables or spread for garlic toasts.

To prepare the sauce, combine eggplant puree with crushed tomatoes in a saucepan over medium heat until warmed through. This recipe will provide enough sauce for up to 1 pound of your favorite-shaped pasta.

Roasted Red Pepper Sauce

3 red bell peppers, 2 if they are very large
2 cloves garlic, popped from skin
2 tablespoons extra-virgin olive oil (a couple of glugs)
A handful of chopped fresh flat-leaf parsley leaves
2 tablespoons tomato paste
Coarse salt and black pepper
1 can (28 ounces) crushed tomatoes

Place halves of seeded red bell peppers skin side up on a cookie sheet as close to the broiler as possible. Broil peppers on high until skins are evenly blackened. Remove from oven and dump the peppers into a paper sack and close it. Let the peppers stand for 5 minutes. Dump peppers out onto a plate. Peel skin away from the meat of the peppers and discard.

Heat garlic and oil in the microwave on high for 20 seconds. Place the peppers, parsley, olive oil, garlic, tomato paste, and salt and pepper in a processor. Pulse until the peppers form a smooth paste. If you stop here, this red pepper paste makes a great topper for sandwiches or garlic toasts, or a dip for carrot, celery, or bread sticks.

To prepare sauce, heat red bell pepper paste and crushed tomatoes in a saucepan. This is enough sauce for 1 pound of pasta.

You Won't Be Single for Long Vodka-Cream Sauce

3 tablespoons, extra-virgin olive oil (three times around the pan)

2 cloves garlic, minced

1 can (28 ounces) crushed tomatoes

20 leaves fresh basil, roughly cut or torn

2/3 cup vodka (a few good glugs)

1 pound linguine or fettuccini

1/4 cup (twice around the pan) heavy cream or half-and-half

Heat olive oil and garlic in a deep saucepan over medium heat. When the garlic speaks, add tomatoes and heat through. Stir in basil leaves. When basil wilts, stir in vodka and bring to a boil. Give the pan a shake and reduce heat to low. Simmer until pasta of choice is cooked until al dente. When you drain the pasta, add the cream to your sauce, then stir in until sauce blushes a shade or two lighter. Toss with hot pasta and serve with bread and a green salad and a nice Chianti. She or he will be yours.

Mamma Elsa's Pasta with Peas, Prosciutto, and Onion

3 cloves garlic, minced

2 tablespoons (twice around the pan) extra-virgin olive oil

2 pinches crushed red pepper flakes

1/4 pound sliced prosciutto di Parma, chopped into narrow strips 2 to 3 inches long (see Note)

Note: Imported prosciutto is available at most deli counters.

1 small white cooking onion, minced or grated

1 can (28 ounces) diced tomatoes

1 can (15 ounces) crushed tomatoes

20 leaves fresh basil, roughly cut or torn

1 cup frozen green peas

1 pound fettuccini or linguine, cooked until al dente

Heat garlic, oil, and crushed red pepper flakes in deep skillet or frying pan over medium heat until the garlic speaks. Add prosciutto and onions and cook another couple of minutes to sweeten the onion. Add tomatoes and basil. When basil wilts, reduce heat to low. Drain cooked pasta. Add peas to sauce. Toss pasta with sauce and dump onto a serving platter. Serves 4 to 6.

The Three R's: Rigatoni, Rapini, and Ricotta Salata Pasta

1 pound rigatoni

4 cloves garlic, minced

2 tablespoons extra-virgin olive oil (twice around the pan)

2 bunches rapini (broccoli rabe) roughly cut into 2-inch pieces, bottom 2-inches discarded

1 can (14 ounces) fat-free chicken broth

A couple shakes nutmeg (1/4 teaspoon)

1 bunch fresh thyme, leaves stripped from stems and chopped (3 to 4 tablespoons)

1/2 pound ricotta salata, crumbled (see Note)

Kosher salt and cracked black pepper, to taste

Start a large pot of salted water to boil. Cook rigatoni until al dente, and drain.

In a large skillet, sauté garlic in oil over medium heat until garlic speaks. Add rapini and cook 3 or 4 minutes. Add broth and nutmeg. Cover pan loosely with foil and cook another 10 minutes or so, until rapini becomes tender. Add drained, rinsed pasta to rapini and broth. Toss with thyme, crumbled ricotta salata, and salt and pepper, to taste. Dump out onto a serving platter. Feeds up to 6 with bread and a salad of chunked tomatoes and sliced onions drizzled with oil.

Note: Ricotta salata is an Italian cheese that tastes like a mild feta and is widely available in specialty cheese cases at many supermarkets.

PRESTO PESTOS

Each recipe will provide enough sauce for 1 pound of pasta.

Method for each recipe:

Toast pine nuts (pignoli), walnuts or sesame seeds until golden brown before using them. (Buy nuts a handful at a time from the bulk bins.)

Heat oil and garlic in small pan on low heat or in microwave, 20 seconds on high, before using.

Pulse all ingredients in a processor or blender until paste forms.

Serve over hot pasta, but never heat the pestos themselves. Pestos should be used at room temperature.

Classic Basil Pesto

1/2 cup extra-virgin olive oil
1/4 pound grated Parmigiano Reggiano cheese
3 ounces pine nuts (a handful)
2 cloves garlic, popped from skin
1 bunch basil, about 40 to 50 leaves

Parsley Pesto

1/2 cup extra-virgin olive oil
1/4 pound grated Parmigiano Reggiano or Romano cheese
3 ounces walnut pieces (a handful)
2 cloves garlic, popped from skin
1 bunch fresh flat-leaf parsley, tops ripped away from stems

Spinach-Walnut Pesto

1/2 cup extra-virgin olive oil
1 cup fresh spinach leaves, packed down, or 1/2 cup drained, defrosted frozen chopped spinach
3 ounces walnut pieces (a handful)
2 cloves garlic, popped from skin
2 pinches ground nutmeg
1/4 pound grated Parmigiano Reggiano or Romano cheese

Sugoloso: Sun-Dried Tomato and Basil Pesto

1/2 cup extra-virgin olive oil
A pinch crushed red pepper flakes
2 cloves garlic, popped from skin
A handful sun-dried tomatoes
20 leaves fresh basil
2 ounces pine nuts (a palmful)

Reconstitute tomatoes by simmering in a little hot water. Drain and cool before using.

Artichoke Crema Pesto

1 cup drained canned artichoke hearts in water
1/2 cup extra-virgin olive oil
2 cloves garlic, popped from skin
A handful fresh flat-leaf parsley
A pinch cayenne pepper
Juice of 1/2 lemon
Coarse salt, to taste

Sesame-Cilantro Pesto

2 tablespoons sesame tahini
1 tablespoon sesame oil
1/2 cup chicken or vegetable broth
2 cloves garlic, popped from skin
A handful fresh cilantro leaves
A pinch cayenne pepper
2 tablespoons (several shakes) soy sauce
2 tablespoons toasted sesame seeds, stirred in after you process the pesto.

GRAN'PA EMMANUEL'S PASTA CONCOCTIONS

Emmanuel Nini's Ziti with Sausage and Cannellini

1/2 pound bulk sweet sausage (see Note)

1/2 pound bulk hot sausage

2 tablespoons extra-virgin olive oil (twice around the pan)

3 cloves garlic, minced

1 small white onion, minced or grated

1 can (28 ounces) crushed tomatoes

1 can (14 ounces) diced tomatoes

20 fresh basil leaves, roughly cut or torn

1 can (15 ounces) cannellini beans, drained and rinsed

1 pound ziti rigate (with lines), cooked until al dente (still slightly firm to the bite)

Note: Bulk sausage is available at the butcher counter.

In a deep skillet or frying pan, break up sausage and sauté crumbles over medium-high heat. Remove from pan to a paper-towel-lined dish to drain. Return the pan to heat. Reduce heat to medium low. Add olive oil, garlic, and onion and cook 5 minutes, until the onion sweetens. Add tomatoes, basil, and beans. Heat through. Return sausage crumbles to sauce. Drain pasta. Combine with sauce and serve with plenty of cheese and bread. Serves 4 to 6.

Manny's Many-Herb Sauce with Walnuts

2 bunches arugula, washed and dried (about 2 cups loosely packed)

4 sprigs fresh thyme, leaves stripped from stems and chopped

3 sprigs fresh oregano, leaves stripped from stems and chopped

10 leaves fresh basil

2 branches rosemary, leaves stripped from stem and chopped

2 sprigs sage

2 sprigs mint

A handful fresh flat-leaf parsley leaves

1 cup chicken broth

1/2 cup white wine

2 bay leaves

A handful walnuts

4 cloves garlic, minced

2 tablespoons extra-virgin olive oil (twice around the pan)

A pinch nutmeg

Coarse salt and black pepper, to taste

1 pound of penne, cooked until al dente

Grind arugula in food processor. Remove it from the processor and set it aside. Add all other herbs, except bay leaves, and pulse them in processor until ground. Place them in a bowl with chicken broth and white wine. Add bay leaves. Next, toast walnuts in a 300° F oven for a few minutes until golden brown. Wipe out the processor and pulse walnuts until coarsely ground.

Heat garlic in oil over medium heat in a large skillet. Add arugula and cook down for 3 or 4 minutes. Sprinkle with a pinch of nutmeg and salt and pepper. Add herbs, broth, and wine. Bring to a boil. Cover, reduce heat to low, and simmer for 10 minutes. Discard bay leaves. Drain pasta. Toss with sauce and sprinkle with toasted nuts.

Manny's Sweet and Sour Sauce

3 cloves garlic

2 pinches crushed red pepper flakes

2 tablespoons extra-virgin olive oil (twice around the pan)

1 small white onion, minced or grated

1 can (28 ounces) crushed tomatoes

1 can (15 ounces) diced tomatoes

A handful jumbo pitted green olives (see Note)

A handful pitted black oil-cured olives

A handful (3 or 4 tablespoons) golden raisins

10 to 15 leaves fresh basil, roughly cut or torn

A handful fresh flat-leaf parsley, chopped

1 pound penne

A handful pignoli/pine nuts (about 3 ounces), toasted

Start salted water to boil for pasta and cook pasta until al dente.

Heat garlic, crushed red pepper, and oil in a deep skillet over medium heat until the garlic speaks. Add minced onion or grate the onion into the pot with a handheld grater. Cook onion for a couple of minutes to sweeten. Add tomatoes, olives, raisins, basil, and parsley. Bring to a boil. Reduce heat to low and let simmer while pasta cooks. Drain pasta and toss with sauce. Top with toasted pine nuts. Feeds 4, well.

Note: Quality olives are available in bulk at the deli counter in many markets — it's a lot cheaper to pay for the handful you need than it is to buy big jarsful.

Sicilian Sausage and Fennel Pasta

3/4 pound bulk sweet sausage
1 bulb fresh fennel, tops and outer layer trimmed away
1/2 medium white onion
3 cloves garlic
A pinch allspice
Black pepper, to taste
1 cup chicken broth
1/3 cup Pernod or Anisette liqueur
1 pound penne, cooked until al dente
3 tablespoons (twice around the pan) heavy cream or half-and-half
Grated Parmigiano Reggiano cheese, for the table

Break up sausage in deep skillet and brown over medium heat. Cut fennel and onion into chunks and process with garlic in food processor or mince by hand.

Add fennel, onion, and garlic to pot. Sprinkle with allspice and pepper. Give the pan a good shake. Add broth. Cover and reduce heat to low. Simmer for 10 minutes, until fennel bits are tender.

Uncover and bring heat up to medium again. Let the broth reduce by half, about 5 minutes. Douse with liqueur. Bring mixture back to a boil. Drain pasta. Add cream to sauce and give the pan a shake. Toss immediately with the pasta. Serve with plenty of grated cheese and extra black pepper.

salads
and other green stuff

Three Too Simple Dressings for Green Salad

Roasted Shallot Vinaigrette

Roasted Garlic Vinaigrette

Lemon and Olive Oil

Bistro Salads

Jackson Salad

Fennel and Parmigiano Salad

Tomato and Onion Salad

Kim's Favorite Fruited Curry Couscous Salad

Macho Gazpacho Salad

Manny's Orange and Oregano Salad

Margarita Melon Salad

Manny's Warm Potato Salad

Salads As Suppers

The Real-Deal, Yes, You Have to Use an Egg,
No Mustard, Hold the Mayo Caesar Salad

Beef Brutus: Sliced Steak on Caesar Salad Greens

Cleo's Chicken Caesar

Mark Antony's Scampi Caesar

Panzanella: Bread and Tomato Salad

Greek Diner Salad

Greek Goddesses Eat at Joe's Chicken Salad

Caprese Salad

Chicken Caprese Salad

Chicken Salad with Figs and Prosciutto

Warm, Leafy Greens

Verdure di Primo Maggio: Greens of the First of May

Rapini and Garlic

Rapini and Sausage

Rapini Chicken Soup

Spinach with Nutmeg and Garlic

Swiss Chard with Golden Raisins

Dandelion Greens and Pancetta

What worries me about bottled dressings is how they work. Creamy dressings that don't require refrigeration . . . oil and vinegar that doesn't separate . . . weird colors like bright orange, pink, and green — dressing, or poster paint? Fat-free dressings are interesting. What's worse for us? Olive oil, or chemically engineered fat substitutes?

Bottled dressings on fresh vegetables — an oxymoron.

The key to dressing greens or vegetables is simple . . . the simpler the dressing, the better the greens and vegetables taste.

Try not to drown your greens. You want to just dress them in a light coat of olive oil and seasoning. Too much of a good thing, spoils it — another lesson on life, via your food.

I am not a fan of trends, but salads as supper is a great idea. If you learn to make a few classics, Caesar and Greek, for example, their variations, with the addition of protein found in sliced meats, fish or shell fish, are endless. For the price of one plate at the new bistro, you can make five nights of salad suppers at *Chez Vous*.

Warm, dark greens are a whole different thing. They provide much more than iron. Greens with garlic and olive oil are a universal soul food. In my family, a pinch of nutmeg is added to any dark green leaf. It brings out a sweet, earthy taste that balances any bitterness left in greens after they have wilted.

Eating dark greens is like savoring a fine wine. The flavors seem simple, but the aftertaste is complex. A plate of rapini, spinach, escarole, collards or chards will restore your soul. Make some. Eat some. Share some. They're a good deed, indeed.

THREE
TOO SIMPLE DRESSINGS
FOR GREEN SALADS

Roasted Shallot Vinaigrette

Shallots, minced, 1/4 shallot per person

Extra-virgin olive oil, 1 tablespoon per person (once around the bowl)

Balsamic vinegar, 1 teaspoon per person (a couple of shakes)

Heat shallots in oil to infuse their flavor into the oil. I heat mine in an ovenproof bowl when I put my bread in to crust up for dinner. After roasting the oil at 275°F for 10 minutes, the shallots should begin to speak by sizzling in the oil. Remove the dish. Allow the oil to come back to room temperature. Mix in the vinegar with a whisk or fork and toss thoroughly with the greens. You can also throw them in a small dish and heat in the microwave for 15 or 20 seconds if it's too hot to turn on the oven, but the flavor is not quite as intense.

Roasted Garlic Vinaigrette

Substitute 1/2 clove garlic per person for shallot.

Repeat the same method of oven-roasting the garlic in oil before combining with vinegar.

Lemon and Olive Oil

Drizzle dark greens such as baby spinach and dandelion or beet greens with a generous amount of olive oil. Coat the leaves evenly. Squeeze the salad with fresh lemon juice. Sprinkle with coarse salt and toss a second time. Let stand a few minutes to allow the lemon juice to mellow and wilt the greens.

BISTRO SALADS

Jackson Salad

8 ounces spring-mix salad greens

2 tablespoons capers

1/4 red onion, sliced thin

Dressing:

1 teaspoon Dijon mustard

1/4 teaspoon (a couple of shakes) Montreal Steak Seasoning by McCormick

1/3 cup extra-virgin olive oil

1/4 cup white balsamic vinager

2 shakes Worcestershire sauce

Combine greens, capers, and onion in a large bowl. Mix dressing ingredients with fork. Pour evenly over salad. Lightly toss. Feeds 4.

Fennel and Parmigiano Salad

Fresh fennel, tops trimmed and the outer layer of the bulb peeled away

Parmigiano Reggiano cheese, shaved with a knife or a cheese blade

Extra-virgin olive oil

Freshly ground black pepper

> **"Fresh fennel tastes like icy-cold licorice. It's sweet and delicious and complements the salty tang of good, Parmigiano cheese."**

Cut the fennel bulbs in half. Trim out the core with a paring knife. Lay the bulb flat on cutting surface and slice very thin, following along with your free hand gripping the bulb to the board, fingers curled under. Layer the fennel and cheese shavings on a serving dish. Drizzle with green olive oil and top with freshly cracked or ground black pepper.

Tomato and Onion Salad

Firm plum tomatoes, as many you can fit in your belly

Thinly sliced white onion, as close to paper thin as you can get them

Extra-virgin olive oil, a generous drizzle

Fresh flat-leaf parsley, chopped, a generous sprinkle

Coarse salt and freshly ground black pepper

If you like onion, go heavy on it; if not, go easy on it. Drizzle the oil by placing your finger over the top of the bottle to allow a slow stream that you can control. Use only fresh parsley — it's cheap and keeps for days. Mix it all up with your hands, the best utensils you own. Eat this with good, chewy bread. Add a hunk of cheese, and wine or any herbed, oil-dressed or white pasta dish. I envy your first bite.

"This is a staple of Italian and Italian-American life. It is my favorite dish, hands down. Tomato and onion salad was also a cheap, healthy meal on many nights when money was tight. Every time I take a bite, I see my mom or my gran'pa smiling, telling me a story, sitting right next to me at the kitchen table. Try it. You'll be hooked for life."

Kim's Favorite Fruited Curry Couscous

2 cups water

2 tablespoons extra-virgin olive oil (twice around the bowl)

1 tablespoon (half a palmful) curry powder

1 box Near East plain couscous, about 1 1/4 cups

1/4 cup golden raisins

2 navel oranges, one whole, one peeled, sectioned and chopped

4 scallions, sliced thin, on an angle

1 carrot, peeled and grated

Coarse salt, to taste

In a medium, covered saucepan, bring water, olive oil, and curry powder to a boil. Stir in couscous and raisins. Remove from heat and let stand, covered, for 5 minutes. Fluff with fork. Squeeze the juice of 1 whole orange over the dish. Combine the scallions, carrot, and chopped orange sections. Salt, to taste. Dump the sunny mixture out onto a serving dish. Edible flowers, found in the produce department, make a pretty garnish. Serve at room temperature or chilled. Feeds up to 6 as a side dish, 2 to 3 as a lunch or light supper.

Macho Gazpacho Salad

3 firm vine-ripe tomatoes, chopped

1/2 seedless European cucumber, chopped

1 green bell pepper, seeded and chopped

1/2 medium Spanish onion, chopped

A drizzle extra-virgin olive oil (about 2 teaspoons)

Coarse salt and coarse black pepper, to taste

4 shakes Spanish picante sauce or cayenne pepper sauce (Tabasco, Red Hot, etc.)

A palmful fresh chopped cilantro

Juice of 1 lime

Combine vegetables in a bowl. Toss with a little olive oil, salt and pepper, hot sauce, and cilantro or parsley. Squeeze the juice of 1 lime over the salad. The salad is best served cold, like the soup. If you make it ahead, chill just the vegetables. Wait to dress the salad until you are ready to serve it. Serves up to 6 as a side dish or 2 to 3 as a light lunch or late summer supper with crusty bread and Spanish wine.

Manny's Orange and Oregano Salad

Navel oranges, peeled and sliced into rings, rings sliced in half
Red onion, sliced thin and chopped, 1/4 onion for every 4 oranges
Fresh oregano leaves, chopped, 1 stem for every 4 oranges
Extra-virgin olive oil, drizzled
Red wine vinegar, a splash
Coarse salt and black pepper

Combine all ingredients in a shallow bowl. Stick a spoon in it to serve.

Margarita Melon Salad

Cubed honeydew, cantaloupe, or a combination
Nonalcoholic margarita mix
Fresh mint, finely chopped

Douse melons with bottled margarita mix. Sprinkle with fresh mint. Combine and serve. Kick it up with a splash of Midori liquor.

Manny's Warm Potato Salad

2 pounds baby Yukon gold potatoes, or red potatoes, quartered
1/2 cup beef consommé, found in the canned soups section of any market
1/4 cup (a handful) chopped fresh flat-leaf parsley
2 tablespoons extra-virgin olive oil (twice around the bowl)
1 tablespoon (a couple good splashes) red wine vinegar
Coarse salt and black pepper, to taste

Boil potatoes in water for 10 to 12 minutes. Drain and return to hot pot to dry out potatoes. Add room-temperature beef consommé, parsley, oil, vinegar, and salt and pepper. Toss until the consommé is absorbed by potatoes. Serve at room temperature. Serves up to 6.

SALADS AS SUPPERS

The Real-Deal, Yes, You Have to Use an Egg, No Mustard, Hold the Mayo Caesar Salad

2 large cloves garlic

2 anchovy fillets, plus extra for garnish (If you hate anchovies, you won't taste the two in the dressing; read on.)

1/3 cup extra-virgin olive oil

1 egg yolk (see Note)

4 shakes Worcestershire sauce

1 lemon

3 hearts romaine lettuce, which you can buy in the produce section, prewashed and packed

A handful grated Parmigiano Reggiano cheese, plus extra shavings for the table

Cracked black pepper, to taste

> Note: If you're worried about the raw egg, use a splash of pasteurized egg product.

> Croutons:
> Large cubes chewy bread, 4 or 5 per person
> Extra-virgin olive oil
> 1 clove garlic

Pop a clove of garlic from its skin with a whack between the flat of your knife and the cutting board. Rub the surface of a heavy-bottomed skillet with the cracked clove. Leave the clove in the skillet. Place the skillet on the stove over medium-low heat. Coat the bottom with a thin layer of olive oil. Add the bread. Let it hang out, giving the pan a shake now and then, for 20 minutes, or until cubes are golden brown and fragrant.

Rub the sides and bottom of your salad bowl, all the better if it's wooden, with the two garlic cloves you'll use in the dressing. After rubbing the bowl, place the garlic pieces, anchovies, and olive oil in a small saucepan. Heat over medium heat until anchovies melt completely into the oil. When you can no longer see them, their fishy flavor will not be distinguishable — just a nice, subtle, salty but almost nutty presence will remain in the oil. Remove the garlic and discard. (The oil is infused with the flavor of the garlic.) Pour the oil into the bottom of the salad bowl. Separate the egg. Discard the white. Mix yolk into oil with a fork. Add Worcestershire. Roll lemon on counter to release juices. Cut lemon in half and squeeze juice into bowl. Mix vigorously with fork. Coarsely chop the lettuce hearts and dump into bowl. Add cheese, a lot of pepper, and croutons. Coat the delicious mixture completely, tossing and turning the salad several times. Serve with extra cheese and pepper. Feeds 2 as a meal, 4 to 6 as a first or side course.

Beef Brutus: Sliced Steak on Caesar Greens

Season 6 ounces of sirloin per person with a little balsamic vinegar or Worcestershire sauce and Montreal Steak Seasoning, available on the spice aisle, or lots of cracked black pepper. Get a griddle pan or nonstick skillet really hot. Cook meat 4 minutes on each side while you are preparing the salad. Remove from heat and let juices distribute for 5 minutes before slicing. Slice beef very thin against the grain and rest it over the top of the salad.

Cleo's Chicken Caesar

Season one boneless, skinless breast of chicken per person with a teaspoon (a shake) of balsamic vinegar. Rub the vinegar into the chicken to tenderize, and let stand while you preheat a nonstick griddle or skillet over medium high heat. Cook breasts for 4 minutes on each side. Sprinkle skillet with a few tablespoons water and rub chicken around in it on each side. The color you'll get will amaze you. Remove chicken from heat and let stand. When Caesar Salad is ready, slice chicken on an angle and spread it over the salad.

Mark Antony's Scampi Caesar

2 cloves garlic, minced, for each 2 servings

A pinch crushed red pepper flakes

2 tablespoons extra-virgin olive oil (twice around the pan)

5 jumbo shrimp per person, peeled and deveined

A shot white wine for every 2 servings

Heat garlic and crushed red pepper in oil over medium-high heat until the garlic speaks. Add shrimp and cook for a minute on each side, keeping pan moving with vigorous shakes to avoid burning garlic. Douse with a little white wine and dump over the top of Caesar greens.

Panzanella: Bread and Tomato Salad

1/2 loaf crusty, chewy bread (about 8 ounces)

6 firm plum tomatoes, diced

1/4 medium white onion, thinly sliced

A handful pitted oil-cured olives

**1/3 pound crumbled ricotta salata cheese
(available in the specialty cheese case at many markets)**

2 sprigs each fresh rosemary and mint, chopped

A palmful chopped fresh flat-leaf parsley

**1 Italian sweet pepper (cubanelle) or substitute bell pepper,
seeded and chopped**

1/3 cup extra-virgin olive oil (a few good glugs)

3 teaspoons red wine vinegar (a few splashes)

Combine all ingredients except oil and vinegar in a big bowl. Beat oil and vinegar with fork and pour over salad. Combine well and let stand for a few minutes for flavors to combine and bread to soften. Makes 2 suppers, 4 to 6 side or first courses.

Greek Diner Salad

2 cloves garlic, minced
1/3 cup extra-virgin olive oil
Juice of 1 large lemon
A pinch allspice
Kosher salt and cracked black pepper, to taste
2 hearts romaine lettuce, chopped
2 plum tomatoes, diced
1/2 medium red onion, sliced very thin
1/2 seedless cucumber, sliced thin
A handful pepperoncini hot peppers, chopped
A palmful (2 tablespoons or so) chopped fresh oregano
1/4 pound feta or flavored feta cheese, crumbled
A handful pitted, oil-cured or Kalamata black olives

In an ovensafe bowl, cover the garlic with oil. Heat in warm oven or in microwave on high for 30 seconds until the garlic speaks. You are infusing the garlic flavor into the oil by adding heat. Whisk in the lemon juice and allspice, and salt and pepper. Set aside.

Combine the lettuce, vegetables, feta cheese, olives, and oregano in a bowl. Toss with dressing. Serves 2 for dinner, up to 6 as a side or first course.

Greek Goddesses
Eat at Joe's Chicken Salad

4 pieces boneless, skinless chicken breast cutlets
2 to 3 teaspoons balsamic vinegar, rubbed into chicken to tenderize

Heat a griddle pan or nonstick skillet over medium high heat. Cook chicken cutlets for 3 minutes on each side. Douse pan with a splash of water and rub chicken around to pick up color. Remove from heat and slice breasts on the diagonal. Rest on top of the Greek Diner Salad. Eat like a Greek God/ess. Serves 2 for dinner, or 4 as a side dish.

Caprese Salad

Firm vine-ripe tomatoes, sliced into 1/4-inch-thick rounds
Fresh mozzarella or smoked fresh mozzarella, sliced like tomatoes
Fresh basil leaves

Extra-virgin olive oil
Coarse salt and black pepper, to taste

Layer tomatoes, mozzarella, and basil leaves. Drizzle plate with oil. Sprinkle with salt and pepper. Serving suggestion: 1 tomato and 3 slices of mozzarella per person.

Chicken Caprese Salad

4 pieces boneless, skinless chicken breasts
2 to 3 teaspoons (a few good splashes) balsamic vinegar
8 slices firm tomato
8 leaves fresh basil
8 slices fresh mozzarella or fresh smoked mozzarella
Extra-virgin olive oil
Cracked black pepper and kosher salt, to taste

Heat griddle pan over medium high heat. Rub chicken with balsamic vinegar to tenderize. Cook chicken breasts for 4 minutes on each side. Splash pan with a little water and rub chicken around to pick up color and flavor from the pan.

Remove from heat and let stand for 5 minutes to come to room temperature. Top each breast with a layer of tomato, basil, and mozzarella, using 2 pieces of each. Drizzle the entire dish with olive oil and top with black pepper and salt, to taste. Serves up to 4 with crusty bread.

Chicken Salad with Figs and Prosciutto

4 pieces boneless, skinless chicken breasts

1 can (14 ounces) no-fat, low-sodium chicken broth

A handful hazelnuts

4 ounces mixed baby salad greens (a couple handfuls, from the bulk
    bin in the produce department)

6 fresh figs, trimmed and quartered, or 8 dried figs,
    reconstituted by simmering in water for 10 minutes, then
    draining and halving

1/4 pound prosciutto di Parma, sliced thin at the deli,
    then cut into short, wide strips, working across the slices of
    prosciutto

1 teaspoon currant or seedless blackberry jelly or all-fruit spread

3 tablespoons extra-virgin olive oil (a couple of glugs)

A splash balsamic vinegar

Freshly ground black pepper

Place chicken in a skillet and cover with broth. Place skillet over high heat to
bring to a boil. Reduce heat to medium low. Cover and simmer for 12 minutes to
poach chicken through. Drain and let stand at room temperature. While chicken
is cooking, toast hazelnuts in a cake pan or on a cookie sheet in 300°F oven
until golden brown. Pour nuts onto slightly damp towel and rub off skins. Transfer
nuts to a baggie and give them a whack with a blunt instrument to break them
up a bit.

Chunk the chicken. Combine in a shallow bowl with greens, figs, and prosciutto.
Mix jelly, oil, and vinegar with a fork. Drizzle over the salad and lightly toss to
coat. Sprinkle with nuts and black pepper. Feeds 4.

WARM LEAFY GREENS

Verdure di Primio Maggio: Greens of the First of May

4 cloves garlic, minced

4 anchovy fillets

3 tablespoons extra-virgin olive oil (three times around the pan)

1 bag (10 ounces) triple-washed spinach, stems trimmed

1 bunch dandelion greens, escarole, or Swiss Chard

2 tablespoons capers (a palmful)

A pinch ground nutmeg

A handful good green and black olives, pitted (see Note)

Black pepper, to taste

In a large skillet, heat garlic and anchovies in oil over medium heat. When anchovies have completely melted into the oil, the fishy taste will become less distinguishable for those who don't really like the taste of anchovies. Add the greens a few at a time, turning as they wilt down, until all can occupy the pan. Add capers, nutmeg, and olives. Cover. Reduce heat to low and let cook for 10 minutes. Turn off stove. Remove from heat. Transfer to serving platter and serve with lots of crusty bread. Add leftover sausages or chicken chunks and some canned low-salt chicken broth for a hearty greens and meat stew.

Note: Look for quality olives in bulk near the deli of your market.

Rapini and Garlic

4 cloves garlic, minced

2 tablespoons extra-virgin olive oil

2 bunches rapini (broccoli rabe) about 2 pounds, bottom 3 or 4 inches of stems trimmed away

1 cup low-sodium, no-fat chicken broth

Heat garlic in oil over medium heat in a large skillet until garlic speaks by sizzling in oil. Add the rapini, as much as you can fit in pan at a time. Turn and coat with oil as you wilt the greens. Add broth. Bring to a boil. Cover and reduce heat to low. Simmer 10 to 12 minutes to soften the bitterness of the greens. Feeds 2 as a meal, up to 6 as a side course.

Rapini and Sausage

Brown and drain bulk sweet or hot Italian sausage and crumble it into the dish for a simple supper.

Rapini Chicken Soup

Add chunked leftover chicken and an extra can of broth, then top with cheese and croutons or garlic toast for a simple soup.

Spinach with Nutmeg and Garlic

2 cloves garlic, minced

1 tablespoon extra-virgin olive oil (once around the pan)

1 bag triple-washed spinach (10 to 12 ounces), stems trimmed

Coarse salt and black pepper, to taste

2 pinches ground nutmeg

Heat garlic in oil over medium heat. Add spinach and turn in pan until leaves wilt. Sprinkle with salt, pepper, and a couple of pinches of nutmeg — it's delicious with any dark green. Remove from heat and serve warm. Makes 4 side servings.

Swiss Chard with Golden Raisins

1/2 medium white onion, chopped

3 cloves garlic, minced

2 tablespoons extra-virgin olive oil (twice around the pan)

2 bunches chard, red or green, stems trimmed away, tops roughly cut

1/4 cup (a handful) golden raisins, left to soak in 1 cup chicken or vegetable broth

Salt, pepper, and ground nutmeg, to taste

Heat the biggest skillet you've got over medium heat and cook the onion and garlic in oil for a minute or two. Add the greens and turn in pan as they begin to wilt. Add raisins with broth, salt, pepper, and nutmeg. Bring to a boil, reduce heat to low, and cover and cook for 10 minutes. Remove cover and turn greens out onto serving dish. Feeds 2 as supper, up to 6 as a side.

Dandelion Greens and Pancetta

3 cloves garlic, minced

1/2 medium white onion, chopped

2 tablespoons extra-virgin olive oil

2 bunches (around 2 pounds) dandelion greens, stems trimmed, tops roughly cut or torn

1/2 cup chicken broth

1/4 pound pancetta (see Note)

Note: Italian rolled bacon with pepper, available at the deli counter.

Heat garlic and onion in oil over medium heat. Add dandelion tops and turn in oil. Add broth. Cover and simmer for 10 minutes. Chop pancetta into small pieces and brown. Do not overcook. Drain the pancetta crumbles on paper towels. Remove the cover from greens and turn off heat. Mix in pancetta and let stand 5 minutes. Serve with good chewy, crusty bread. Serves 2 as a light supper, up to 6 as a side.

make your own
take-out

Pizzas

Margherita Pizza: Tomato, Basil, and Mozzarella
Puttanesca Pizza: Tomato, Olive, Caper, and Anchovy
Carbonara Pizza: Bacon, Egg, and Cheese
Winter Greens Pizza

Sandwiches

Super Sub Balls and Pigskin Potatoes
Antipasto Pie
Chicken Not-Pot-Pie
My Monte Cristos
Chicken Clubs
Greek Wraps with White Bean Hummus
Paninis
Salad Subs

Tex-Mex in No Time

My Sister Ria's Favorite Fajitas
Southwestern Chicken and Black Bean Burritos
Taco Pockets
Macho Mix and Match Enchiladas
Sauces and Fillings
Dilly of a Quesadilla
Spicy Chicken Tacos

Indian & Asian Take-Out

Thai It, You'll Like It Chicken

Moo Shu Pork Pockets with Jasmine Rice Sundaes

Sesame Noodles

Cashew! God Bless You Chicken

No-Pain Lo Mein

Funky Fried Rice

Pot-Sticker Pockets

Shrimp Toast with Cucumber Salad

Curry in a Hurry

Better Burgers

Alaska Burgers

Sweet Sausage Burgers with Grilled Peppers and
Pickled Vegetable Relish

Blue Moon Burgers

Shish-Ka-Burgers

Barbecued Beef and Bean Burgers

Barbecued Beef and Bean Bacon Burgers

Meatza Pizza Burgers

Curried Turkey Burgers

Turkey Loco Burgers with Chunky Guacamole

Hawaii Burgers

Bog Burgers

You're in rush-hour traffic, anyway. You take a detour from your normal route, look for a spot in the lot at the chicken shack, the gourmet food court, or the Tex-Mex restaurant on Main. You make your way in, maneuver into line, break into a sweat when you're asked for your order, wait for the order wishing you'd ordered something else, pay a cashier up to six times the actual value of the food before they "prepared" it for you. You shuffle back out to the parking lot, get back in your car, drive home, carry all your junk inside, plop the sack of food on the counter, put your sweats on, play the messages on the machine, unpack the food, reheat the food, plate the food. Finally, you eat the food. How good was it? Did it taste fresh and healthy? Did you spend the next forty minutes wishing you hadn't eaten it? What time is it? That late, already?

How long does it take you to get take-out?

Take-in takes a lot out of us as well. What happens when you call for a delivery from the Pizza-Pacer or The General Tso Mobile? Do you spend the thirty minutes you wait for it and the thirty after you eat it obsessing about the grease, the fat, the hour of night you're eating? Does one thought lead to another and spiral you into the abyss, questioning every choice you've made in life, from the high school electives you took through to your prom date and up to your skills as a parent, a worker, and a mate? Do you sign up for another membership to the disco-gym downtown the next day?

Knock it off. If we're going to eat Tex-Mex, burgers and pizza, let's enjoy it—before, during, and after. Spend half an hour in the grocery store one lazy Sunday afternoon with a short list made from a few quick recipes. Pick and plan a couple of meals with overlapping ingredients lists to cut down on your shopping time. Commit to cooking. It only takes half an hour. The food will be as good for you as it tastes. You'll spend the next thirty minutes after dinner thinking about all the possibities there are in life. Eat good. Feel good. Make your own take-out.

PIZZAS

Margherita Pizza: Tomato, Basil, and Mozzarella

10 to 15 leaves fresh basil, roughly cut or torn
2 firm vine-ripened tomatoes, thinly sliced
Extra-virgin olive oil
One 12-inch Boboli thin-crust pizza
1/2 pound fresh mozzarella or smoked fresh mozzarella, thinly sliced

Combine basil and slices of tomato in a shallow dish and drizzle with olive oil. Arrange slices of tomatoes and basil in a thin layer across the top of the pizza. Dot the pie with several disks of thinly sliced fresh mozzarella or fresh smoked mozzarella. You will have the best luck slicing the mozzarella with a small, straight-edged knife with a thin blade — slice it right from the fridge, the colder it is the better.

Place the pizza in a cold oven directly on the center rack or on a perforated pizza pan. Turn oven to 400°F and leave the pie in for 12 minutes. Remove and serve immediately with extra olive oil for drizzling and crushed red pepper flakes or freshly ground black pepper. Feeds 2 with salad as supper or cut into 16 slices for cocktail parties of up to 8.

Puttanesca Pizza: Tomato, Olive, Caper, and Anchovy

2 cloves garlic, cracked and peeled with a good whack against the cutting board using the flat of your knife

1/8 teaspoon (a pinch) crushed red pepper flakes

2 tablespoons extra-virgin olive oil (twice around the pan)

2 anchovy fillets

1 can (14 ounces) tomatoes, drained and diced

One 12-inch thin-crust Boboli pizza shell

2 tablespoons (a palmful) chopped fresh flat-leaf parsley

2 tablespoons capers, drained (available in the international foods aisle of your market)

1/4 cup pitted Kalamata olives, drained and coarsely chopped (also available in the international aisle)

1/2 cup grated blended Italian cheeses (see Note)

A perforated pizza pan can be had for 6 to 12 dollars in most supermarkets. I recommend the small investment for anyone who likes crisp crust.

Mince garlic. In a small skillet, working over medium heat, sauté garlic and crushed red pepper flakes in oil until the garlic speaks by beginning to sizzle. Add anchovy fillets and use the back of a wooden spoon to help melt the anchovies into the oil. Once dissolved, the anchovies' taste will mellow and serve only to give the sauce a nutty flavor and provide natural salt in the finished pizza.

Note: Available in resealable pouches, sold in the dairy section — there is a six-cheese blend available in most stores that packs a lot of flavor and includes provolone, Asiago, mozzarella, and Romano cheeses. Many stores also carry reduced-fat cheese blends.

Add diced tomatoes to the skillet, and coat them evenly with flavored oil. Remove from heat.

Place the pizza crust on the pizza pan. Sprinkle evenly with tomato mixture out to the edges of the pizza shell. Add the parsley, capers, and olives to the pizza in the same manner. Fluff up the cheese blend in the sack it comes in by running your fingers through it. Cheese blends save time but often become clumped by hanging out in the dairy case or in a sack on your car's backseat for too long. Cover the pie with a light layer of the cheese right out to the edges. Some of the colors of the toppings should still peek through. Too much cheese will result in a soggy pie.

Place pie in oven directly on center rack or on perforated pizza pan. Turn oven to 425°F. Cook pie at least 8 minutes before checking on it and no more than 12 minutes altogether. Cheese should begin to brown and edges should be crisp when you remove the pizza from the oven.

Serves 2 as a meal with a salad and up to 8 as an appetizer or party food.

> ❝Puttanesca is a pasta sauce named for streetwalkers, or ladies of the night, as it is spicy, fast, and easy to make. This pizza packs the same strong flavor as the pasta dish and it's quicker to make than it is to call Domino's.❞

Carbonara Pizza: Bacon, Egg, and Cheese

2 cloves garlic, minced

Extra-virgin olive oil

2 eggs

4 slices pancetta (see Note)

One 12-inch thin-crust Boboli pizza shell (available in the Italian foods aisle of the market)

A handful chopped fresh flat-leaf parsley

1/2 pound fresh mozzarella or fresh smoked mozzarella

Freshly ground black pepper

In a small non-stick skillet, heat garlic in a little olive oil, just enough to coat the bottom of the pan, over medium heat. Beat eggs and scramble with garlic and olive oil until eggs are fluffy but not dry. Transfer eggs to a small dish and set aside. Wipe pan with paper towel and return to heat. Chop pancetta and toss into skillet. Brown pancetta bits but do not crisp them too much — they will continue to cook on top of the pizza. Transfer bits to paper towels to drain. To assemble pizza, scatter the scrambled egg bits across the surface of the shell. Sprinkle generously with pancetta or bacon pieces and a little chopped fresh flat-leaf parsley. Dot pie with thin disks of sliced fresh mozzarella or smoked mozzarella.

Place the pizza in a cold oven directly on the center rack or on a perforated pizza pan. Turn oven to 400°F and leave the pie in for 12 minutes. Remove and top with a little freshly ground black pepper. Feeds 2 with salad as supper or cut into 16 slices for cocktail parties of up to 8.

Note: Italian meat similar to bacon, rolled with black pepper. This product is widely available at the deli counter of many markets — chopped center-cut bacon slices may be substituted.

Winter Greens Pizza

2 sprigs fresh thyme

1 cup part-skim ricotta cheese

Salt and pepper, to taste

2 cloves garlic, minced

Extra-virgin olive oil

8 ounces mixed winter greens (about 4 big handfuls) — Swiss chard, spinach, escarole, choose one or combine as few or as many as you like, but trim away big veins/stems before you cook them.

A pinch ground nutmeg

One 12-inch thin-crust Boboli pizza shell

1 cup grated blended Italian cheeses (see Note, page 78)

Strip thyme from stems and combine with ricotta, and salt and pepper. Set aside. In a small skillet over medium heat, cook garlic in a little olive oil, just enough to coat pan — drizzle it once around the pan. When the garlic speaks, add as many greens to pan as will fit and turn as they wilt down; add more until all greens are evenly coated and wilted. Sprinkle with nutmeg. If you are using bitter greens, cover and reduce heat to lowest setting and cook for 5 minutes to mellow. If you are using spinach, remove from heat once wilted.

"This pie looks like snow-covered evergreens. Yummy for snuggling by a fire and watching *Casablanca* again, Sam."

To assemble, spread the crust first with an even layer of ricotta. Scatter wilted greens, using tongs or a fork, over the ricotta. Give the greens a bit of a shake over the skillet as you remove them, leaving the liquid in the pan — you don't want a soggy pie. Sprinkle the greens with an even layer of grated Italian cheeses.

Place pie in cold oven directly on center rack or on perforated pizza pan. Turn oven to 400°F and cook 12 to 15 minutes or until cheeses melt and just start to brown. Serves 2 as supper, or get 16 cuts for cocktail parties of up to 8.

SANDWICHES

Super Sub Balls and Pigskin Potatoes

1 1/2 pounds lean ground beef
1 egg
1/2 teaspoon (a shake or two) crushed red pepper flakes
3 cloves garlic, minced
1/4 medium Spanish onion, minced
A handful chopped fresh flat-leaf parsley
1 cup Italian bread crumbs (a couple of good handfuls)
4 shakes Worcestershire sauce
2/3 pound provolone cheese, cut into 16 small cubes
Olive oil for brushing baking sheet

Quick Marinara:
3 cloves garlic, minced
2 tablespoons extra-virgin olive oil
2 pinches crushed red pepper flakes
2 cans (28 ounces each) crushed tomatoes
15 to 20 leaves fresh basil, roughly cut or torn
2 sprigs fresh oregano, leaves stripped from stem and chopped
A handful chopped fresh flat-leaf parsley

4 sesame-seeded sub rolls

Preheat your oven to 425° F.

Combine meat, egg, red pepper flakes, garlic, onion, parsley, bread crumbs, and Worcestershire in a bowl. Pull a palmful of meat mixture into your hand. Nest a piece of provolone in the middle of the meat and form a ball. Place on a nonstick cookie sheet brushed with a little olive oil. Repeat until mixture is gone, about 16 balls later. Place cookie sheet in oven and bake for 12 to 15 minutes.

For Quick Marinara, in a deep frying pan or saucepot, heat garlic in oil over medium heat with red pepper flakes until garlic speaks by sizzling in oil. Add tomatoes and herbs. Bring to a boil, reduce heat, and simmer over low heat until ready to serve.

Drop the stuffed sub balls into sauce. Scoop up sauced sub balls into rolls and serve with oven fries and/or a simple salad.

The traditional sub is made with fried meatballs and covered with melted, salty, sorta-mozzarella cheese product. This is not only better tasting, by comparison, it's good for you.

Pigskin Potatoes

Cut white or scrubbed Idaho potatoes lengthwise into thin wedges. Allow 1 potato per person. Toss potato wedges into a big bowl and coat with a little olive oil. Sprinkle with Montreal Steak Seasoning, a spice blend by McCormick, or salt, pepper, paprika, and garlic powder. Pour wedges out onto a cookie sheet. Roast for 20 minutes in 425°F oven. If preparing with above subs, throw potatoes in oven first, then add meatballs to oven and cook together for last 12 to 15 minutes.

Antipasto Pie

1 large round loaf of good, chewy bread (from the fresh-baked goods section of the market)

1 jar giardiniera salad, available in Italian foods aisle (see Note)

A handful chopped fresh flat-leaf parsley

1/4 pound sliced capocollo

1/4 pound sliced prosciutto cotto (see Note)

1/4 pound sliced Genoa salami

1/3 pound sliced provolone cheese

2 roasted red bell peppers, four halves, jarred, or see recipe for Roasted Red Pepper Sauce on page 43

Pitted black oil-cured and jumbo green olives (see Note)

1/4 pound washed mixed greens (from the bulk bin in the produce section)

Extra-virgin olive oil

> Note: Citterio makes a nice prosciutto cotto rubbed with rosemary, available at many deli counters. Olives are available in bulk bins near deli counter; get a scoop or two of each. Giardiniera Salad is a mixture of pickled vegetables and hot peppers.

Cut off the top of the large round loaf of bread. Cut into bread about an inch, an inch and a half, from the crust. Cut into and around the loaf, stopping just short of the bottom. Scoop out all the guts of the loaf of bread. Discard, or save them for tomato and bread salad, page 64, or toast them and grind them up for bread crumbs.

Drain the jar of giardiniera and dump the salad into your food processor with the parsley. Pulse to coarsely chop.

> "This is a great thing to make for tailgate parties, office pot lucks, school functions or living room picnics on video rental night."

Cover the bottom of the hollowed loaf with giardiniera relish. Fill bread with layers of meats, cheese, roasted peppers, olives, and greens. Drizzle a little olive oil into and over the loaf. Top with the lid of the loaf of bread. Press down to pack everything in. Use a big, sharp knife to cut the pie into wedges. Serves 4 to 6 as supper, up to 12 as party food.

Chicken Not-Pot-Pie

4 pieces boneless, skinless chicken breasts

2 branches fresh rosemary, leaves stripped from stem and chopped

Salt and freshly ground black pepper, to taste, or crushed red pepper, to taste

2 teaspoons (a splash) balsamic vinegar rubbed into chicken to tenderize

1 large, round loaf crusty peasant bread, top cut off and inside scooped out

1 can artichoke hearts in water, drained

2 whole (4 halves) roasted red bell peppers, jarred, drained (or see page 43)

1/4 medium Spanish onion, sliced thin

2 plum tomatoes, sliced

1/4 pound sliced provolone, smoked provolone, or rustico with red pepper cheese

A handful pepper salad, pepperoncini, or pepper rings

Baby greens or baby spinach

Extra-virgin olive oil

Heat a griddle pan over high heat. Cook chicken, coated with rosemary, pepper, and balsamic, for 5 minutes on each side. Remove from heat.

Place the chicken in the bottom of the hollowed-out loaf of bread. Pile any antipasto combination you like on top — artichokes, peppers, onions, tomatoes, cheese, pepper salad, greens, etc. Drizzle olive oil down through the pie. Sprinkle with salt and pepper or crushed red pepper, to taste. Place the lid back on the bread. Cut into wedges and serve. Feeds up to 12 as an appetizer, 4 as dinner.

My Monte Cristos

2 eggs

A splash milk

A pinch ground nutmeg

Coarse salt and black pepper, to taste

1 loaf sliced English muffin bread or old-fashioned white bread

1/2 pound honey-roasted turkey breast

1 Granny Smith apple, washed and sliced very thin

1 brick smoked cheddar cheese, 1/3 pound minimum, cut into thin slices

A pat butter

Heat a nonstick griddle or large frying pan to medium high. Scramble eggs with milk, nutmeg, salt, and pepper.

Assemble four sandwiches by topping a slice of bread with a slice of turkey, a slice or two of apple, and a thin layer of cheddar cheese. Put top slices of bread in place and press down lightly on each sandwich.

Melt a pat of butter on the grill. Quickly coat each sandwich by turning it in egg batter. Drop sandwiches directly on the griddle, placing them as close together as possible — you want to cook all 4 sandwiches at once, if possible. Flip after 4 or 5 minutes. The other side will brown even more quickly, a minute or two.

Remove from heat and quarter each sandwich by cutting from corner to corner. Makes 4 sandwiches, 16 quarters.

Chicken Clubs

8 slices center-cut bacon
4 pieces boneless, skinless chicken breasts
4 toothpicks

Topping: Tomato and Onion Salad
3 plum tomatoes, thinly sliced into rings
1/4 medium white onion, minced
Chopped fresh flat-leaf parsley, a palmful leafy tops
Salt and pepper, to taste
A drizzle extra-virgin olive oil
Romaine or Bibb lettuce leaves
Crusty kaiser rolls

Crisscross two pieces of bacon on a cutting board. Place a piece of chicken in the center of the cross. Wrap bacon up and over breast. Place a toothpick through the center of the bacon-crossed chicken breast to keep in place while cooking. The chicken will resemble hot crossed buns. Heat griddle pan over medium high heat or use an outdoor grill and cook chicken for 6 to 7 minutes on each side, until bacon is crisp and brown and chicken is not fleshy to the touch.

While chicken cooks, combine tomatoes and onion with parsley, salt, and pepper. Drizzle with olive oil.

Top each roll bottom with a chicken breast. Remove toothpick in breast and top with tomato mixture, lettuce leaf, and roll top. Makes 4 sandwiches.

Greek Wraps with White Bean Hummus

1 can (15 ounces) cannellini beans, drained and rinsed
2 stems fresh rosemary, leaves stripped from stem and chopped
1 clove garlic
Extra-virgin olive oil
Black pepper, to taste

2 firm vine-ripened tomatoes, quartered and thinly sliced
1/4 seedless cucumber, halved, then thinly sliced
1/4 medium red onion, sliced thin
A handful pitted Kalamata olives
A handful chopped fresh flat-leaf parsley
1/4 pound mixed greens (from the bulk bin in the produce
   department)
1 lemon
Extra-virgin olive oil
Coarse salt, to taste
1/4 pound feta cheese, crumbled

4 large pita breads, or flour tortilla wraps, or flavored wraps

Combine beans, rosemary, garlic, a touch of olive oil, and black pepper in a food processor or blender. Pulse until mixture is smooth.

Combine tomatoes, cucumber, parsley, greens, and the juice of 1 lemon in a bowl. Drizzle with olive oil, and sprinkle with salt. Combine well.

Warm pitas or wraps in oven or on a griddle pan. Spread with a generous dose of white bean hummus. Top with a layer of Greek salad mixture. Sprinkle with feta cheese crumbles and roll. Wrap lower half of wraps with foil or waxed paper to keep it together while you eat your way down. Keep a paper towel in your hand as you eat to catch and drips. Feeds up to 4. Batches of the white bean spread are also a terrific dip for specialty potato chips, celery, or bread sticks. Make a half portion of the salad for 1 or 2 wraps and save the extra white bean spread for dipping snacks.

Panini

The Bread

To make these warm wonders, drizzle a little olive oil in the bottom of a nonstick skillet. Place two pieces of sliced Italian bread in the pan for each panini. Lightly toast the first side, flip the bread over, and cover with a thin layer of filling — some classy classic combinations are listed below. Close the sandwich up like a grilled cheese and toast the outside to your taste. Quarter your paninis and serve them right off your cutting board for a party treat, or with a simple salad for light supper.

The Fillings

☐ Thinly sliced fresh mozzarella or smoked mozzarella and prosciutto di Parma

☐ Mozzarella or smoked mozzarella, capocollo, and a little hot pepper relish or hot pepper rings

☐ Sliced smoked mozzarella or smoked provolone, sliced tomato, and fresh basil leaves

☐ Provolone, slices of roasted red pepper, and arugula

☐ Crisp bacon or pancetta, arugula, and sliced tomatoes (an Italian BLT)

☐ Grilled, sliced portobellos, arugula, and smoked mozzarella or smoked cheddar cheese

"Paninis are thin Italian sandwiches, sometimes grilled in a sandwich press. The fillings are not piled high, just evenly."

Salad Subs

Recipes for Caesar salad and Greek salad are given in the second section of this book. For a simple supper, split a loaf of Italian bread, hollow it out, and toast the shells under the broiler until lightly browned. Fill up the super-size sub with Caesar or Greek salad, put the top on, and hack it up into big chunks to share with up to 4 for dinner, or as many as 12 for cocktail parties.

TEX-MEX IN NO TIME

My Sister Ria's Favorite Fajitas

Marinade:

3 tablespoons liquid cayenne pepper sauce (Red Hot or Tabasco)

2 tablespoons ground cumin (half a palmful)

1 teaspoon allspice

2 tablespoons chili powder (half a palmful)

A handful fresh oregano and thyme leaves combined, the yield of 3 or 4 stems of each

1/2 bottle of beer

A drizzle extra-virgin olive oil

The Guts:

1 1/2 pounds flank steak, or 4 boneless, skinless chicken breasts (8 pieces)

Extra-virgin olive oil

1 large Spanish onion, cut in half and then into 1/2-inch strips

1 red bell pepper, seeded and cut into 1/2-inch strips

1 green bell pepper, seeded and cut into strips

2 poblano chiles, cut into strips (If none are available in your market, use Cubanelle Italian long peppers.)

Salt and pepper, to taste

The Topping:

Pico di Gallo, the peck of the rooster, is fresh salsa made of only finely chopped tomato, serrano or jalapeño chiles, minced onion, cilantro, mint, and salt. The mint curbs the bitterness of the cilantro.

The Wraps
8 small, 6-inch flour tortillas or 4 large, 9- to 12-inch tortillas

Mix all marinade ingredients together.

Coat the meat or poultry in the marinade and let it hang out. Heat two pans, a nonstick griddle to high, a nonstick frying pan to medium high. Drizzle the frying pan with oil. Cook the onions, peppers, and chiles, with an occasional shake, until they darken around the edges, about 5 minutes. Sprinkle with salt and pepper and turn off heat.

Drop meat or chicken onto the very hot griddle pan or a second skillet. Sear for 2 minutes on each side. Remove from heat. Slice very thin, on the bias, and return strips to griddle to brown and cook through. Drop cutting board and knife into sink to sanitize.

Heat tortillas according to package directions. Fill with sizzling meat or chicken, veggies, and a scoop or two of *Pico di Gallo*. Wrap and chow down. Serves up to 4 with refried beans and beverage of choice (margaritas or mockaritas are not a bad choice).

Southwestern Chicken and Black Bean Burritos

4 pieces boneless, skinless chicken breasts (2 full breasts)

1 teaspoon each ground cumin and chili powder

A couple shakes cayenne pepper sauce

1 tablespoon (once around the pan) extra-virgin olive or corn oil

1/2 medium Spanish onion, chopped

2 cloves garlic, minced

1 can black beans, drained and rinsed

3 tablespoons (a couple of glugs) smoky barbecue sauce

Kosher salt and cracked black pepper, to taste

1 heart romaine, shredded

6 green onions, thinly sliced

2 tomatoes, seeded and chopped

Four 10- to 12-inch flour tortilla wraps, flavored or plain (see Note)

Note: Flour tortillas are often sold in the dairy aisle of the market.

Rub chicken with cumin, chili powder, and cayenne sauce. Heat griddle pan to high. Cook the chicken breasts 4 minutes on each side and remove from heat.

While chicken is cooking, heat a skillet over medium high heat. Go once around the pan with oil. Cook onions and garlic until onions are soft, about 5 minutes. Add beans and barbecue sauce. Chop cooked chicken breasts and drop into barbecued beans. Heat mixture through. Season with salt and pepper, to taste.

Pile chicken and beans onto tortilla. Top with lettuce, green onions, and tomatoes. Wrap and roll. Serve with chips and salsa. Makes 4 large burritos.

Taco Pockets

1 pound ground beef

1/2 medium Spanish onion, grated

2 teaspoons water

2 tablespoons (a good palmful) ground cumin

2 tablespoons chili powder

A shake or two cayenne pepper or Red Hot sauce

1 teaspoon garlic powder

Kosher salt, to taste

Four 12-inch plain or flavored flour tortilla wraps

1/2 pound Monterey Jack, pepper Jack, cheddar, or smoked cheddar cheese, grated

1 heart romaine lettuce, shredded

1 large, firm tomato, chopped

Chopped fresh cilantro (optional)

Combine the beef with onion, water, and all the seasonings except the salt. Form into 4 patties.

Heat a nonstick skillet over medium high heat or fire up the grill. Cook burgers 4 to 5 minutes on each side. Salt to your taste. Place each burger in the center of a tortilla wrap. Top with cheese, lettuce, tomato, and cilantro. Wrap the tortilla up and over the burger on all 4 sides.

KIDS LOVE THESE!

Flip square-shaped packet over and cut from corner to corner, making 2 taco pockets. Serve with chips, salsa, or refried beans and rice.

Macho Mix and Match Enchiladas

Pair any 1 of 3 sauces with any 1 of 4 fillings in less than half an hour. The only trick is to read through the instructions and figure out how best to overlap cooking times — what can you be doing while the other pot is simmering? Think it out before you cook, and half an hour becomes all the time in the world.

Enchiladas are a groovy party food as well. Place 8 to 12 enchiladas in a big casserole, top with cheese, and brown under broiler. Add chips and salsas and a pitcher of margaritas and you've got a fiesta.

Sauces

Each recipe serves 4, topping up to 8 enchiladas. Choose from:

☐ **Encinada Enchilada Red Sauce**

☐ **Warm Salsa Verde**

☐ **Quick Mole Sauce**

Fillings

All recipes will fill up to 8 enchiladas.

☐ **Mexican Pulled-Chicken Filling**

☐ **Beef or Pork Filling**

☐ **Black Bean Filling**

Tortillas

Use soft corn tortillas for enchiladas, about 7 to 8 inches in diameter. They are available in the refrigerated cases of most any market. To heat tortillas, wrap in aluminum foil and place in the oven at 275°F until the fillings and sauce are ready.

Cheeses

To top any of the enchiladas, try a blend of grated Mexican cheeses that is available in resealable pouches in the dairy aisle. I like one that combines asedero, Monterey Jack, cheddar, and queso fresco cheeses.

How to Assemble Enchiladas

Scoop a little sauce onto the bottom of a casserole dish or shallow serving platter.

To make an enchilada, place a scoop or two of filling down the center of a tortilla shell and roll. Place filled tortillas seam side down into sauce on platter or casserole. Line up tortillas, one next to another, and top with remaining sauce and grated cheeses. Melt cheeses under broiler and serve immediately.

SAUCES

Encinada Enchilada Red Sauce

1 clove garlic, minced
1 tablespoon (once around the pan) extra-virgin olive oil
1 small white onion, grated
1 can (28 ounces) pureed tomatoes
1 tablespoon dark chili powder (half a palmful)
A pinch ground cinnamon
1 teaspoon (a couple of good pinches) ground cumin
Coarse salt, to taste

Heat garlic in oil over medium heat. When it speaks by beginning to sizzle, add the onion by grating it directly into the pot. Cook onion and garlic for 2 minutes to soften and sweeten the onion. Add pureed tomatoes and seasonings. Bring to a boil, then reduce heat to low and keep warm until enchiladas are ready to top.

Use red sauce on any enchilada — chicken, beef, pork, or bean.

Warm Salsa Verde — A Spicy, Green Dream

12 tomatillos, husked and halved (widely available in the produce section of your market)

2 cloves garlic, minced

1 tablespoon (once around the pan) extra-virgin olive oil

1 small white onion, grated or minced

1 jalapeño, seeded and minced

1 can (14 ounces) chicken broth

1 teaspoon (a couple of pinches) ground cumin

Coarse salt, to taste

1 avocado, ripe to the touch (giving to your finger with mild pressure)

A little chopped fresh oregano — the leaves off one or two stems (optional)

Salsa Verde is traditionally paired with chicken or pork filled enchiladas. "

Place the tomatillos in a food processor and pulse to a coarsely ground paste.

Heat garlic in oil over medium heat. When the garlic speaks by beginning to sizzle, grate onion with a hand grater directly into the pot. Add jalapeño. Heat onion and jalapeño through for a minute or two and add the ground tomatillos. Simmer tomatillos with onion for 5 minutes. Add the chicken broth and seasonings.

Halve the avocado with the skin on by cutting in and down to the pit all the way around the avocado. Separate the avocado halves and scoop out the pit with a large spoon.

Scoop the flesh out of the skins and into the pot. Mush up the flesh into chunks with the back of a fork. Stir the avocado into the sauce to thicken it up a bit. Return sauce to a low boil; reduce heat to warm until enchiladas are assembled.

Quick Mole Sauce, a. k. a. I Never Thought I'd Like It, But It Really Is Good and I Don't Taste the Chocolate Sauce

1 clove garlic, minced

1 tablespoon (once around the pan) extra-virgin olive oil

1 small white onion, grated or minced

1 can (28 ounces) tomato puree

Chopped fresh oregano (the leaves off one or two stems, chopped, about 1 teaspoon)

1 tablespoon dark chili powder (half a palmful)

1 teaspoon ground cumin

A pinch allspice

Coarse salt, to taste

1/2 ounce unsweetened chocolate (half of one square)

Real mole sauces are a combination of ground peppers and chocolate, can take up to 4 days to prepare, and can come in almost any color. This is a tomato-based sauce, reddish brown in color, that will give you the taste of many moles.

Heat garlic in oil until it speaks by beginning to sizzle. Add onion by grating it directly into the pot using a hand grater. Cook onion for a minute or two to sweeten. Add tomato puree. Heat through. Add seasonings and chocolate. Stir constantly until the chocolate melts into sauce. Reduce heat to warm and keep sauce warm until enchiladas are ready.

Mole is often paired with chicken. I think it's best with black bean or beef enchiladas.

FILLINGS

All recipes will fill up to 8 enchiladas.

Mexican Pulled-Chicken Filling

4 pieces (2 full breasts) boneless, skinless chicken
1 lime
1 small onion, quartered
1 bay leaf
2 stems fresh oregano
1 can (14 ounces) no-fat chicken broth
1 cup water
Coarse salt, to taste
2 tablespoons tomato paste
1/2 teaspoon each (a pinch or two) ground cumin and chili powder

Rub chicken breasts with the juice of 1 lime to tenderize. Place chicken in a pan with next 5 ingredients. Bring to a boil, reduce heat to medium, and poach for 15 minutes. Drain and transfer chicken to a bowl. Discard oregano stems, bay leaf, and onion. Shred up chicken with 2 forks. Add tomato paste, seasonings, and a bit of salt. Work the paste through the chicken evenly. To reheat this mixture, add a touch of chicken broth or water to a small pan and simmer filling for a minute or two.

Big batches of this freeze well. Defrost the filling on your way to work and throw a Mexican dinner together in minutes that night.

See assembly directions, page 95, for enchiladas. Top with any of the above sauces and cheese. Melt cheese under the broiler to brown. Serve with a simple green salad or rice and beans.

> This chicken filling can be used in soft tacos, tostadas, burritos, or enchiladas. The chicken is poached, resulting in a mild taste; it's flavorful but not hot. The spice and heat will come out of the sauces and toppings you pair it with.

Beef or Pork Filling

For up to 8 enchiladas, four servings.

1 1/2 pounds ground beef or ground pork
2 cloves garlic, minced
1 small white onion
1 cup beef broth, for beef filling only
1 cup chicken broth, for pork filling only
1 tablespoon chili powder (half a palmful)
1 teaspoon ground cumin (a few good pinches)
A pinch allspice
2 tablespoons tomato paste, for use in beef filling only

Brown beef or pork in hot pan over medium-high heat. Add garlic. Grate onion with a hand grater directly into the pot. Cook for a minute or two to sweeten onion. Add broth and seasonings. If you are making beef filling, add paste. Simmer until liquid reduces by half, about 10 minutes. Mixture should not be too wet.

Black Bean Filling

For up to 8 enchiladas, four servings.

2 cloves garlic, minced
1 tablespoon extra-virgin olive oil (once around the pan)
1 small white onion
1 jalapeño, seeded and minced
2 cans (15 ounces each) black beans, drained but not rinsed
1 teaspoon ground cumin (a few good pinches)
2 tablespoons tomato paste
Coarse salt, to taste

Heat garlic in oil until it speaks. Grate onion into the pan with a hand grater. Add jalapeño. Cook for a minute or two. Add beans and mush up a little with the back of a fork. Stir in cumin and tomato paste and season with salt, to taste.

Top beans when wrapping with shredded smoked cheddar and green onions for a really special enchilada.

Dilly of a Quesadilla

2 pieces boneless, skinless chicken breasts

1/2 pound chorizo (Spanish smoked sausage), or substitute andouille, linguica, or spicy kielbasa

1 tablespoon smoky barbecue sauce

8 large flour tortillas

12 ounces shredded Mexican cheese blend (see Note)

Note: Asedero, Monterey Jack, and cheddars. Available in the dairy aisle of your market.

Salsa:

6 firm plum tomatoes, diced

1/4 medium white onion, chopped fine

A palmful cilantro leaves, finely chopped

1 serrano pepper, seeded and minced (see Note below)

Coarse salt, to taste

Note: Serranos look like tiny jalapenos and are widely available in produce sections.

Combine all salsa ingredients.

Heat griddle or nonstick skillet to high. Cook chicken and chorizo for 4 minutes on each side. Remove from heat. Dice chorizo and chicken.

Coat the chicken by combining it with barbecue sauce in a small bowl.

Wipe off griddle and return to medium-high heat. Blister each tortilla for 30 seconds on the first side, then flip. Place a little chicken, chorizo and cheese on 1/2 of the tortilla's surface. Fold the flap formed over the top of the meat and cheese. Press down with a spatula. Flip the half-moon-shaped quesadilla over and cook for another 30 seconds. Remove.

Cut each quesadilla into 4 wedges and top with a sprinkle of salsa. Repeat. Each quesadilla should only be on the grill for 2 minutes or so. Makes 8 quesadillas.

Spicy Chicken Tacos

1 1/2 pounds boneless, skinless chicken breasts, cut into small cubes

1 tablespoon extra-virgin olive oil (once around the pan)

1 small onion, chopped

1 cup tomato puree

2 teaspoons chili powder (half a palmful)

1 teaspoon ground cumin (half as much as chili powder)

A handful coarsely chopped Spanish olives stuffed with pimientos

A handful golden raisins

Coarse salt, to taste

8 jumbo corn taco shells, or 8 flour tortillas for soft tacos

1 clove garlic, minced

Toppings:

☐ Shredded cheeses (smoked cheddar, Monterey Jack, or pepper Jack)

☐ Avocado dices

☐ Tomato dices

☐ Chopped green onion

☐ Shredded lettuce

Brown chicken in olive oil in a big skillet over medium heat. Add onion and garlic and cook another couple of minutes to soften onion. Dump in tomato puree, seasonings, olives, raisins, and salt, to taste. Bring to a bubble, reduce heat to low, and simmer until ready to serve. Warm taco shells or flour tortillas in oven according to package directions. Scoop filling into shells and top at the table. Feeds up to 6 with a chunked vegetable or green salad.

INDIAN AND ASIAN TAKE-OUT

Thai It, You'll Like It Chicken

Start a box of jasmine rice, following the directions for 4 to 6 servings, before you begin. The rice will take 25 minutes, the chicken only 20.

2 tablespoons (once or twice around the pan) sesame, peanut, or vegetable oil

1 pound boneless, skinless chicken breast, cut into thin strips

1 red bell pepper, cut into 1/4-inch strips

3 to 4 cloves garlic, minced

1 serrano hot pepper, seeded and minced (Serranos look like mini jalapeños)

4 tablespoons hoisin sauce (Asian sauce found near soy sauce)

2 tablespoons Thai fish sauce (see Note)

1 teaspoon (a good pinch) sugar

1/4 cup water (a splash or two)

1 cup loosely packed basil leaves (the yield of one good bunch)

Jasmin rice, cooked

In a wok or large nonstick skillet, heat sesame oil over high heat till hot. Stir-fry chicken for 4 minutes. Add red bell pepper, garlic, and serrano. Cook for 2 or 3 minutes. Add hoisin, fish sauce, sugar, and water. Throw in basil and toss until it wilts. Dump out onto a bed of jasmine rice. Garnish with any extra basil leaves. Feeds up to 4, well.

Note: Available in the Asian foods section. If you cannot find it, use a few shakes of soy sauce.

Moo Shu Pork Pockets

1 1/2 pounds ground pork

1/2 cup sliced water chestnuts, chopped (the yield of 1 can of sliced chestnuts, approximately 7 ounces, drained)

2 cloves garlic, minced

1/4 teaspoon (two pinches) cayenne pepper

12 gingersnap cookies (about 3/4 cup — the hard ones, processed into crumbs or smashed up in a baggie with a blunt instrument)

2 tablespoons (several shakes) soy sauce

1 egg

1 jar hoisin sauce, found in the Asian foods aisle of the market

1 package fresh bean sprouts from the produce section, or 1 can (12 ounces), drained

1 bunch (8 to 10) green onions, sliced thin on a diagonal

1 carrot, grated

A palmful chopped fresh cilantro

Six 12-inch flour tortillas/wraps (found in the dairy section of the market)

Combine pork and next 6 ingredients in a bowl. Form mixture into 8 patties.

Heat a griddle pan or large nonstick skillet over medium-high heat. Grill 4 pork patties at a time for 4 minutes on each side. Heat tortillas according to package directions or heat up a second skillet or griddle over high heat and blister each tortilla for 30 seconds per side.

To assemble, brush a tortilla with hoisin sauce. Pile some bean spouts, green onions, and carrot in the center of each tortilla. Sprinkle with a little chopped cilantro. Top with a pork pattie. Wrap the tortilla up and over on all sides, forming a square. Flip the stuffed tortilla over, cut from corner to corner, forming 2 moo shu pockets. This recipe will make 16 pockets from 8 burgers and will feed 4 to 6 people. For parties, place 4 toothpicks in each burger wrap and cut the packets into quarters, yielding 32 pieces.

Jasmine Rice Sundaes

Cook jasmine rice according to the directions on the box. Serve with an ice cream scoop. Drizzle scoops of rice with soy sauce and duck sauce from the packets you've saved from all the Chinese take-out you've ordered since you moved in. Top with toasted sesame seed "sprinkles. "Yummy! — Jasmine Rice Sundaes. Toasted sesame seeds can be found in the Asian foods aisle of your local market.

Sesame Noodles

1/4 cup low-sodium soy sauce

2 tablespoon-size scoops tahini (see Note)

2 tablespoons (twice around the bowl) toasted sesame oil (found in Asian foods aisle)

2 pinches cayenne pepper

2 cloves garlic, minced

1 inch gingerroot, grated, or 2 pinches ground ginger

1 pound cappellini (angel hair pasta) cooked until al dente

3 scallions, sliced thin on an angle

1 large carrot, peeled and grated

Toasted sesame seeds and crushed red pepper flakes to garnish

Note: A paste made from ground sesame seeds — tahini can be found in the international or whole/natural food aisles of your local market.

Combine soy sauce, tahini, sesame oil, cayenne, garlic, and ginger root in a bowl. Whisk until dressing is smooth.

When pasta is cooked until al dente (still slightly firm to the bite), drain it and run it under cold water until noodles are chilled. Drain the cooled noodles well — give them several good, strong shakes.

Dump noodles into a big bowl with the dressing and combine until noodles are evenly coated with a thin layer of sauce. Add veggies and dump noodles onto a serving dish. Garnish with sesame seed sprinkles and a little crushed red pepper flakes. Serves 4 for a lunch or light supper with fruit or a chunked vegetable salad or up to 8 as a side dish or party offering.

Cashew! God Bless You Chicken

1 box jasmine rice

1 pound of boneless, skinless chicken breast, diced
Combine chicken in bowl with:
  1 tablespoon (once around the bowl) sesame oil
  2 cloves garlic, minced and mashed
  2 tablespoons (a couple of glugs) rice wine, rice vinegar,
    or dry sherry
  A couple of shakes crushed red pepper
  Black pepper, to taste
Set it aside and let it hang out.

1 tablespoon sesame oil
1 large carrot, peeled and diced into small cubes
1 red bell pepper, seeded and diced
1 can (about 7 ounces) sliced water chestnuts, drained and coarsely
  chopped
3 heaping tablespoon-size scoops hoisin sauce (see Note)
A couple handfuls unsalted cashews (from the bulk candy and nuts
  section of the market)
3 green onions, thinly sliced on an angle

Following directions on box, start rice.

Heat oil in wok or large nonstick skillet over high heat until it smokes. Add carrot and stir-fry for 2 or 3 minutes. Add the coated chicken and cook another 3 or 4 minutes. Toss in the bell pepper and chestnuts. Heat through for 1 minute. Add the hoisin and toss to coat evenly. Dump chicken out over a bed of jasmine rice and top with cashews and green onions. Feeds 4 well.

Note: An Asian condiment, similar to barbecue sauce, easily found in many markets in the Asian foods aisle.

No-Pain Lo Mein

1 pound spaghetti, cooked until al dente

1/2 to 3/4 pound boneless, center-cut pork, or chicken breast, cut into very thin strips

2 tablespoons (twice around the pan) toasted sesame oil

3 tablespoons vegetable oil (three times around the pan)

A couple shakes of crushed red pepper flakes

1/4 pound snow peas (a couple of handfuls)

1 small onion, peeled and thinly sliced

1 cup bean sprouts (the yield of one 7-ounce can) drained, or 2 handfuls fresh sprouts

3 green onions, thinly sliced on an angle

2 tablespoons soy sauce

Coarse salt, to taste

While pasta is cooking, brown meat in wok or large skillet over high heat in 1 tablespoon sesame oil. Remove from pan.

Add vegetable oil and crushed red pepper. Stir-fry snow peas, onion, and bean sprouts for 1 minute. Remove from pot with a slotted spoon and add to meat.

Dump drained, cooled pasta into wok. Add green onions and half your cooked meats and veggies. Toss and fry the mixture until noodles and veggies are combined. Drizzle with a couple tablespoons soy sauce and 1 tablespoon sesame oil. Combine well. Sprinkle with salt, to taste. Dump onto serving dish and top with remaining meat and veggie bits.

Funky Fried Rice

2 cups of water

1 cup enriched white rice

2 tablespoons sesame oil

1/2 pound boneless center-cut pork chops, cut into thin strips, or
  1/2 pound boneless, skinless chicken, cut into thin strips

1/2 red bell pepper, chopped

2 green onions, thinly sliced on an angle

2 eggs, scrambled with black pepper to taste

1 tablespoon vegetable oil

2 tablespoons (several shakes) soy sauce

2 pinches crushed red pepper (a couple of shakes)

2 pinches ground ginger

1 cup fresh bean spouts (found in organic produce section)

1 cup (a couple of handfuls) frozen baby peas

1/2 cup (about 1/4 pound) chopped baby shrimp (300 count)

1/2 cup toasted sliced almonds to garnish

Boil water. Add rice. Reduce heat to simmer. Cover and cook 12 to 15 minutes, until liquid is absorbed. Dump rice onto a shallow plate to cool it down. Place rice in refrigerator until ready to use in the dish. Rice can be prepared the night before, as well. Leftover white rice is the best for fried rice.

Heat 1 tablespoon sesame oil in wok or shallow, big nonstick skillet until oil is very hot and begins to smoke. Add meat and cook for 4 minutes — keeping the meat bits moving is important for even cooking. Remove meat.

Add bell pepper and green onions and heat through for a minute. Pour in eggs and scramble with veggies until eggs are set. Remove eggs.

Add 1 tablespoon sesame oil and vegetable oil to wok or skillet. Add cool or cold rice. Sprinkle with 2 tablespoons soy sauce, crushed pepper, and ginger as the rice fries. Return meat and egg bits to wok. Add bean sprouts and peas and chopped baby shrimp. Combine rice, meat, and veggies well. Top with toasted almonds for crunch and serve right from the wok or pan. Feeds up to 6.

Pot-Sticker Pockets

1 1/2 pounds ground pork

1/2 cup (a good handful) chopped water chestnuts

2 green onions, chopped

2 tablespoons soy sauce (several good shakes)

1/2 teaspoon ground ginger or 1-inch piece fresh gingerroot, grated

2 cloves garlic, minced

A pinch crushed red pepper

1/2 orange (Grate the outer skin into bowl, then juice the orange into mixture.)

8 large flour tortillas

Topping:

2 teaspoons honey

1/4 cup white vinegar

1 cucumber, seeded and peeled, thinly sliced

1/2 carrot, shredded

> "These pork-burger sandwich pockets taste like a giant Chinese dumpling. This recipe makes up to 8 pockets."

Hoisin sauce (available in the Asian foods aisle of the market)

Bibb lettuce leaves, shredded

Combine pork and next 7 ingredients in a bowl. Form into patties and cook for 5 minutes on each side on grill pan or outdoor grill over medium-high heat or hot coals. As burgers cook, baste with sauce.

Mix honey and vinegar and coat cuke and carrot in the dressing. Wash and dry one head Bibb lettuce leaves. Shred by thinly slicing.

To heat all 8 flour tortilla wraps, wrap in a slightly damp paper towel, then in foil, and place packet in 325°F oven or on grill until burgers are done. To heat individually, get a big skillet or another griddle really hot and blister the tortillas for 15 seconds on each side — no oil necessary.

To assemble, paint tortilla with hoisin. Place a palmful of lettuce in center of tortilla. Top with a couple of scoops of the shredded carrot and cucumber mixture, and 1 pork pattie. Wrap tortilla up and over on all 4 sides and flip entire square-shaped packet over. Cut in half from corner to corner, forming two pockets.

Shrimp Toast with Cucumber Salad

1/4 pound baby shrimp (300 count)

3 eggs

1 tablespoon cornstarch

1 inch fresh gingerroot, grated, or 2 pinches ground ginger

2 tablespoons (twice around the pan) vegetable oil

2 teaspoons (a drizzle) toasted sesame oil (found in the Asian foods aisle of the market)

6 slices white toasting bread, crusts trimmed

Grind the shrimp into a paste in a food processor. Scramble the eggs in a shallow bowl with cornstarch and ginger. Combine ground shrimp with egg mixture.

Heat 1 tablespoon vegetable oil and a drizzle of sesame oil in a large nonstick skillet over medium-high heat. Coat 3 slices of bread at a time in egg-and-shrimp mixture. Cook in hot pan for 2 minutes on each side to brown. Repeat process for next 3 slices. Cut each slice of shrimp toast into 4 triangles by slicing from corner to corner. Serve with cucumber salad to top.

> "A terrific first or side course and fun for parties, this recipe will make 6 slices, or 24 triangles."

Cucumber Salad

2 teaspoons honey

1/4 cup white vinegar

1 cucumber, seeded and peeled, thinly sliced

A few sprigs fresh cilantro, finely chopped

A pinch coarse salt

Combine honey and vinegar. Coat cucumber evenly with dressing. Sprinkle with cilantro and salt.

Curry in a Hurry

No coconut milk, lower in fat, big flavor.

Curry is actually a blend of several spices. In addition to curry powder, curry pastes are available in grocery stores on the international foods aisle. I prefer using the paste for texture and taste.

Traditional condiments for curry include toasted coconut and chopped toasted peanuts. Some lower fat condiments are on facing page.

Jasmine or white rice

4 pieces boneless, skinless chicken breasts or thighs or combination of both, cut into chunky pieces and dusted with a handful all-purpose flour

1 yellow medium Spanish onion, peeled, halved, and cut into 1/4-inch strips

1 piece fresh gingerroot, about 2 inches, grated

3 cloves garlic, minced

1 can (15 ounces) no-fat, low-sodium chicken broth

3 tablespoons mild curry paste

A handful (about 1/4 cup packed) golden raisins

2 to 3 tablespoons mango chutney (found in the condiment aisle of the market or 1/4 cup mincemeat (found in the baking goods aisle)

2 tablespoons peanut or sesame oil (twice around the pan)

Coarse salt, to taste

Start a pot of water to boil for jasmine or white rice, following the directions on the box for 4 to 6 servings. The rice will take longer than the dish to prepare.

In a large skillet, working over medium-high heat, brown the chicken for 4 minutes on each side in the peanut or sesame oil. Remove chicken from pan and set aside.

Add onion, gingerroot, and garlic. Sauté for another 3 minutes, until the onion becomes tender. Add broth and lift off all of the good junk stuck to the bottom of the pan. Add curry paste and raisins. Return chicken to the pan. Heat through to a boil. Give the pan a good shake. Reduce heat to medium low. Stir in chutney to thicken and sweeten. Simmer for 5 to 10 minutes to desired thickness.

Serve with condiments and white or jasmine rice. Feeds 4 with warm flat breads like lavosh or pita.

Condiments

Serve any combination of the following as toppings for your curry dish:

- ☐ Spanish peanuts
- ☐ Chopped cilantro
- ☐ Mango chutney
- ☐ Chopped green onion
- ☐ Orange segments
- ☐ Edible flowers
- ☐ Coconut flakes
- ☐ Pineapple chunks

BETTER BURGERS

Alaska Burgers

1 pound 93% lean ground beef

1/2 medium Spanish onion, minced or processed

4 shakes Worcestershire sauce

1/4 teaspoon allspice (1 good pinch)

1/2 teaspoon ground cumin (two good pinches)

Cracked black pepper

1/3 pound (minimum) brick of smoked cheddar cheese, cut into 1/2-inch slices

4 fresh, crusty onion rolls

Thick-sliced tomato and lettuce to top

Mix beef, onion, Worcestershire, allspice, cumin, and black pepper in a bowl. Separate a quarter of the mixture. Take a slice of the smoked cheese and place it in the middle of the mixture. Form the pattie shape around the cheese filling. Patties should be no more than 3/4-inch thick. Repeat with rest of mixture, to have a total of 4 patties.

Heat a nonstick griddle or frying pan to medium hot. Cook burgers 5 to 6 minutes on each side. Meat should be cooked through and cheese melted. Check each burger with an instant-read thermometer for an internal temp of 170°F for well done if undercooking concerns you. Or cut into one and check the color of the meat.

Salt burgers after preparation to your taste. (Salting beef before cooking draws out juices and flavor.) Top with tomato slices and lettuce. Serves 4.

Sweet Sausage Burgers with Grilled Peppers and Pickled Vegetable Relish

1/2 pound bulk sweet sausage
1/2 pound lean ground beef
4 long, sweet, red or green Italian peppers (cubanelle)
Extra-virgin olive oil
8 ounces giardiniera salad (see Note)
A handful fresh flat-leaf parsley leaves
1 lemon
4 round, crusty, sesame-seeded rolls, split

If cooking outside, light charcoal or heat gas grill to medium high. Combine bulk sausage with beef and form into quarter-pound patties.

Brush whole peppers with olive oil and grill or broil until charred all over, 8 to 10 minutes.

Place patties alongside peppers and cook over fire or under broiler for 5 or 6 minutes on each side. Burgers can also be cooked in a skillet over medium-high heat for same amount of time.

While burgers and peppers are cooking, finely chop drained giardiniera with the parsley. When all the vegetables and herbs are minced and combined, squeeze the juice of 1 lemon on the salad. Dump relish into a serving dish.

Remove the peppers from the flame. Quarter the peppers and discard stems.

Pile the sausage burgers into their buns and top with pepper sections and a generous mound of relish. Feeds 4, with simple salad of tomatoes and onions or mixed greens.

Note: Pickled cauliflower, carrots, and peppers, available in jars, found in the Italian foods section of your market.

Blue Moon Burgers

1 pound lean ground beef
4 shakes Worcestershire sauce
Cracked black pepper
1/4 pound blue cheese, cut into 4 pieces
1/4 cup dry red wine
Kosher salt, to taste
4 crusty rolls or toasted sourdough bread

Sliced red onion and romaine lettuce as toppers

Season beef with Worcestershire and black pepper. Take a quarter of the beef in your hand. Nest some blue cheese in the meat and form a pattie around the filling — keep the burgers no more than 3/4-inch thick.

Pour the wine into a shallow dish. Turn each burger in wine and let rest while you heat a nonstick griddle to medium hot. Cook burgers 4 minutes on each side. Check the internal temperature with a thermometer if you have one — 160° F is medium. Salt the burgers to your taste. Place burgers on rolls or bread and top with red onion and romaine. Serves 4.

Shish-Ka-Burgers

2 cloves garlic, popped from skin and left whole

Extra-virgin olive oil

1 green bell pepper

1 medium Spanish onion, cut into 1/2-inch-thick slices

2 portobello mushroom tops

1/2 pound ground beef

1/2 pound ground lamb

4 shakes Worcestershire sauce

2 cloves garlic, minced

Montreal Steak Seasoning, or coarse salt and cracked black pepper, to taste

4 crusty rolls, split

Heat whole garlic in enough oil to cover cloves over grill flame or on stovetop in a small pan or bowl. Heat garlic until it speaks by sizzling. Remove and discard the cloves. Using a pastry brush, brush whole pepper, sliced onion, and portobello tops with a little oil and grill until charred on both sides, up to 8 or 10 minutes total time.

Combine beef, lamb, Worcestershire, and minced garlic. Form into patties. Sprinkle with Montreal Seasoning and grill, over medium-high gas flame or charcoal, for 5 or 6 minutes on each side.

Slice portobello tops 1/4-inch thick. Quarter peppers, discarding stems. Halve onion slices. Pile burgers on buns with peppers, onions, and mushrooms. Serve with chunked vegetable salad. Feeds 4.

Barbecued Beef and Bean Burgers

1 cup canned pinto beans, drained and rinsed
1 pound lean ground beef
3 tablespoons smoky barbecue sauce
2 cloves garlic, minced
1/4 medium Vidalia or Spanish onion, grated
Cracked black pepper, to taste
4 shakes Worcestershire sauce

6 crusty rolls
Lettuce and tomato for garnishes

Mush up beans a little with the back of a fork in a deep bowl. Combine beans and beef with barbecue sauce, garlic, grated onion, pepper, and Worcestershire sauce. Form mixture into 6 patties. Cook over outdoor grill or over medium-high heat on a griddle pan on the stovetop. Cook burgers for 6 minutes on each side. Serve on crusty rolls with lettuce and tomato. Add corn on the cob and chunked vegetable salad for a full meal. Feeds up to 6.

Barbecued Beef and Bean Bacon Burgers

Follow above method until patties are formed.

Take 12 slices of thick, center cut bacon or peppered bacon, trim an inch off the fattier of the ends, and discard or save for Sunday omelets. Wrap 2 pieces of bacon around each burger, forming a crisscross in the center of both sides. Fasten the bacon strips into place with a toothpick driven through the center of each burger and out the opposite side. The burgers should look like hot cross buns.

Cook burgers on an outdoor grill if you can, so as much fat as possible will drip away. Cook bacon burgers for 7 to 8 minutes on each side, until bacon is brown and crisp and barbecue burgers have a rich, reddish-brown color. Serve on buns with lettuce and tomato slices, corn on the cob, and chunked vegetable salad.

Meatza Pizza Burgers

3/4 pound very lean ground beef
2 tablespoons tomato paste
1/4 pound chopped chorizo or pepperoni
Chopped fresh oregano, to your taste
2 cloves garlic, minced
Black pepper, to taste
4 slices provolone cheese

Romaine lettuce
1 firm tomato, sliced
4 round, crusty, sesame-seeded rolls

Combine ground beef, tomato paste, chorizo or pepperoni, oregano, garlic, and pepper. Form into 4 patties. Cook burgers for 5 minutes on each side over medium-high gas heat or charcoal. In the last minute, melt a slice of provolone on each burger. Serve with romaine and sliced tomato on crusty rolls. Feeds 4 with a chunked vegetable salad.

Curried Turkey Burgers

1 pound ground turkey
2 tablespoons curry powder
2 shakes Worcestershire sauce
2 cloves garlic, minced
1/4 onion, grated
Chopped cilantro — a palmful
Coarse salt, to taste

4 crusty, round rolls
Bibb lettuce
Thinly sliced red onion
Mango chutney (see Note)
Terra Chips (see below)

Note: Mango chutney is found in the condiments section of the market. Major Grey's and London Pub are the common brand names I've found. Chutney is often served with curries and is a delicious topper for this burger.

Combine turkey with curry powder, Worcestershire, garlic, grated onion, cilantro, and a little salt. Form 4 patties. Grill over medium-high gas heat or charcoal for 5 to 6 minutes per side. Serve on crusty rolls with Bibb lettuce, red onion, and mango chutney. Feeds 4, with Terra Chips.

Serve with funky chips from the natural foods aisle. Try Terra Chips — root-vegetable, multicolored, seasoned chips. Terra Chips is a brand name as well as a product name. The Terra Chips selection includes garlic-and-herbs or salt-and-vinegar Yukon gold chips, spiced taro root chips, and spiced or barbecued sweet potato chips. All of the Terra Chips products are lower in saturated fats than potato chips."

Turkey Loco Burgers with Chunky Guacamole

1 pound ground turkey
1 teaspoon ground cumin
Chopped fresh oregano — a handful of leaves
1/4 onion, grated
Juice of 1 lime
A few shakes hot pepper sauce (Red Hot or Tabasco)
Coarse salt and cracked black pepper, to taste

Chunky Guacamole:
2 avocados, peeled and pitted
1/4 medium Spanish onion, grated
1 jalapeño or serrano hot chile pepper, minced (from the bulk
    variety pepper bins in the produce section)
Coarse salt, to taste
1 plum tomato, seeded and diced

4 crusty rolls, split
Romaine lettuce

Combine turkey and next 6 ingredients. Form into 4 patties and grill over medium-high gas heat or charcoal for 6 minutes on each side.

While the burgers are cooking, mash the avocados with onion, chile pepper, salt, and tomato — leave it chunky.

Place each burger on a bun and pile it with chunky guacamole and a piece of romaine. Feeds 4 with tortilla chips and a summer salad of tomatoes and onions.

Hawaii Burgers

2 pounds ground turkey breast

1/2 teaspoon (a good pinch) ground ginger, or 1-inch piece grated fresh gingerroot

2 tablespoons low-sodium soy sauce

2 cloves garlic, minced

2 green onions, chopped

1/2 cup hoisin sauce (found in the international foods aisle)

2 teaspoons sesame oil (found in the international foods aisle)

1 cored fresh pineapple (available in a pouch in the produce section, cut into rings)

Fresh-baked buns or rolls

1 head Bibb lettuce

Mix turkey with ginger, soy sauce, garlic, and onions. Form into patties and cook for 5 minutes on each side on grill pan or outdoor grill over medium-high heat or hot coals. As burgers cook, baste with hoisin mixed with sesame oil. Grill pineapple rings alongside burgers or in a separate skillet. Place burgers on buns or rolls and top with pineapple rings and Bibb lettuce leaves. Makes up to 8 patties.

Bog Burgers

1 1/3 pounds ground turkey breast

1/2 medium white onion

2 sprigs fresh thyme, stripped from stems and chopped

Coarse salt and black pepper, to taste

1 loaf English muffin bread (from fresh-baked-goods section of market), or old-fashioned toasting bread (from packaged breads section)

1 can (15 ounces) whole berry cranberry sauce

1/4 medium red onion, minced

A handful chopped fresh flat-leaf parsley

1 head of Bibb lettuce, washed and dried

Place turkey in a bowl and grate the onion with a hand grater right into the bowl. Add thyme, and salt and pepper. Mix and form into 6 patties. Heat skillet or grill pan over high heat. Cook burgers 4 minutes on each side. Toast 12 slices of bread. Mix cranberries, onion, and parsley. Top each slice of toast with a burger and lettuce. Spread a scoop of cranberry relish on the top slices of toast and glue into place. Makes 6 bog burgers. Serve with corn on the cob or oven fries and sliced fresh apples and pears.

30-minute
comfort
foods

Mediterranean Comforts

Mini-Meat Patties

Quick Marinara Sauce

Zesty Chicken Cutlets Parmigiana

Emmanuel Nini's Caponata

Mini-Meatball Soup

Pasta e Fagioli

Quick Chick and Noodle

Minestra: Greens and Beans Soup

Minestrone: BIG Beans and Greens Soup

Stracciatelle: Italian Egg Drop Soup

My Sister Ria's Lazy Chicken, or My Lazy Sister Ria's Chicken

My Friend Frank's Favorite Chicken

Tex-Mex One Pots

Quick Chili Con Carne . . . on the Tex Side

Quick Chili Con Carne . . . on the Mex Side

Chili Con Queso

Cajun Chili

White Lightning Chili

Who Ya Callin' Chicken? Chunky Chicken White Chili

Three-Bean Chili

Sorta Posole: Pork and Corn Stew

Sundance Beef Pot Pies

Quick Bread "Lids" for Chilis and Stews

Continental
Favorites

The kitchen has always been and remains the heart of my home. I am safe and calm in this room. I do more than cook and eat good food here — I visit on the phone, do my bills, read the paper, relax.

My mamma is one of ten children born to a stone mason. To say they were poor would be a generous and kind description. Still, to hear her tell you the stories of the food, the family, the good times, you would think her a princess of great privilege.

"The joys of the table belong equally to all countries and times."

Think about the most creative people you've ever met. It's a good bet that many of them came from poor or lower middle-class backgrounds. When the money is tight, all we can give is of ourselves. Through the preparation of good food, the sincere expression of kind words, the storytelling that causes belly-laughs or salty tears, or even the treasuring of keepsakes that makes a house feel like a home, these are the experiences in which we find that heart-filling good stuff that makes us feel whole.

It does take some effort. Willingness is most of the battle. So many young men and women lament to me that they are just too tired to cook. There is a difference between mental and physical fatigue. If you are out working on construction jobs for ten hours, you may need a twilight-time nap. If you are exhausted by the nincompoop quotient at your office, putting on some music and cooking up something good, will make you feel better than plopping down on the sofa to watch syndicated Seinfeld, while waiting for the Pizza-mobile to arrive.

If you have a family, it's worth remembering that frozen dinners and fast food will cost you three or four times the money and rob you of the soul-food you'll get from making a meal for yourself and your kids.

Our grandparents worked hard and were often tired. But at the end of a long day, they were as hungry for the intimacy found around the kitchen table as they were for food on the stove. Be inspired by their example, and fill your own home with the warmth that shared, home-cooked meals can bring.

Here are some of my favorite comfort food recipes to get you started.

MEDITERRANEAN COMFORTS

Mini-Meat Patties

1 1/2 pounds ground beef, pork, and veal (Ask for meat loaf mix at the butcher counter.)

1 cup (a couple handfuls) Italian bread crumbs

2 eggs

1/2 cup low-fat milk

A handful chopped fresh flat-leaf parsley

1/2 cup grated Parmigiano Reggiano or Romano cheese

Freshly ground black pepper, to taste

A handful toasted, chopped pignoli nuts or toasted chopped walnuts

2 cloves garlic, minced

1/2 white onion, grated with hand grater into mixing bowl

1 tablespoon extra-virgin olive oil (once around the pan)

Mix all of above, except olive oil, in a bowl and form into 16 small patties. Heat olive oil in large skillet or frying pan over medium heat. Cook 8 patties at a time, 3 or 4 minutes on each side. When all the patties are done, return the first 8 to the pan and cover with homemade marinara sauce or your favorite brand of pizza sauce. Serve mini patties alongside a little pasta tossed with a dab of butter or olive oil and cheese, or with crispy garlic-toasted rounds of good Italian bread. If you're serving pasta, try a new shape that the kids might go for — like spaghetti wheels (a. k. a. radiatore) — it's my niece Jessie's favorite. Feeds up to 6 with a green salad.

Quick Marinara Sauce

3 cloves garlic, minced

2 tablespoons extra-virgin olive oil

2 pinches crushed red pepper flakes

2 cans (28 ounces each) crushed tomatoes

15 to 20 fresh basil leaves, roughly cut or torn

2 sprigs fresh oregano, leaves stripped from stems and chopped

A handful chopped fresh flat-leaf parsley

Heat garlic in oil over medium heat with red pepper flakes until garlic speaks by sizzling in oil. Add tomatoes and herbs. Bring to a boil, reduce heat, and simmer over low heat until ready to serve.

Zesty Chicken Cutlets Parmigiana

1 pound spaghetti

Juice of 3 lemons, or several tablespoons bottled lemon juice

1/3 cup (a good handful) freshly grated Parmigiano Reggiano or Romano cheese

1 cup (a couple handfuls) Italian bread crumbs

Freshly ground black pepper, to taste

A pinch crushed red pepper flakes

A handful chopped fresh flat-leaf parsley

2 cloves garlic, popped from skin and left whole

3 tablespoons extra-virgin olive oil (three times around the pan)

2 pounds boneless, skinless chicken breast cutlets

1 pound fresh mozzarella or fresh smoked mozzarella, thinly sliced (see Note)

Quick Marinara Sauce

3 cloves garlic, minced

2 pinches crushed red pepper flakes

2 tablespoons extra-virgin olive oil

2 cans (28 ounces each) crushed tomatoes

15 to 20 leaves fresh basil, roughly cut or torn

2 sprigs fresh oregano, leaves stripped from stem and chopped

A handful of chopped fresh flat-leaf parsley

Start a big pot of salted water to boil for pasta. When ready to cook pasta, cook it until it's al dente, or still slightly firm to the bite.

Throw your sauce together by heating garlic and crushed red pepper in olive oil over medium heat. When the garlic speaks by sizzling in the oil, add tomatoes and fresh herbs. Bring to a bubble, reduce heat, and let the sauce hang out over low heat while you prepare cutlets.

Squeeze lemon juice into a shallow dish. Mix Parmigiano, bread crumbs, black pepper, red pepper, and parsley on a large plate. Turn each cutlet in lemon juice, then press and coat in breading.

Heat 2 whole cloves garlic in olive oil in a large skillet or frying pan over medium heat. When garlic sizzles, remove cloves and sauté chicken cutlets for 4 minutes on each side. When the cutlets are done, arrange on an ovenproof serving dish covered with a layer of sauce. Dot each cutlet with a little more sauce and a slice of fresh mozzarella. Place platter under broiler to just melt cheese.

Note: If you've yet to try fresh mozzarella, please let this be your reason. Look for it in the specialty cheeses case at your local market. Fresh mozzarella is more widely available than ever.

Take warm platter right to the table. Toss drained spaghetti with remaining sauce and serve as a side dish. Enjoy!

Emmanuel Nini's Caponata

3 cloves garlic, minced

1/2 teaspoon crushed red pepper (a pinch or two)

3 tablespoons extra-virgin olive oil (two or three times around the pan)

1 palmful golden raisins (about 1/4 cup packed)

1 red bell pepper, chopped

1 green bell pepper, chopped

1 medium Spanish onion, chopped

1 medium eggplant, chopped (peeled or skin-on)

1 celery heart, chopped

1/4 pound green and black olives, pitted

3 tablespoons (a palmful) capers

Kosher salt, to taste

1 can (32 ounces) diced tomatoes

1 can (13 ounces) crushed tomatoes

A handful chopped fresh flat-leaf parsley

3 ounces (1 bottle) pine nuts (pignoli), toasted in oven until golden

In a deep skillet or pot, working over medium heat, simmer garlic and crushed red pepper in oil until the garlic speaks. Add raisins, peppers, onion, eggplant, celery, olive, capers, and kosher salt. Cover pan and cook the vegetables down, stirring occasionally, until eggplant begins to break down, about 7 to 10 minutes.

Add tomato products and parsley. Heat through. Turn off heat. Serve caponata hot or cold as an appetizer or an entree with bread, or tossed with pasta. Sprinkle with toasted nuts when ready to eat.

> "Many recipes for caponata include sugar and/or vinegar; this is not one of them. My gran'pa Emmanuel said that the sweet and sour come out of the ingredients naturally, the sweet from the red peppers, onions, and raisins, the sour from the capers, eggplant, and parsley. If your grandparents put vinegar and/or sugar in, please make them happy and add some."

Mini-Meatball Soup

"For the mini meatballs in your life."

1 pound lean ground beef

1 egg

1/2 cup Italian bread crumbs

1/3 cup grated Parmigiano Reggiano cheese (a couple handfuls)

1 teaspoon garlic powder

1/2 medium Spanish onion, chopped, plus 1/4 onion, minced

Freshly ground black pepper and salt, to taste

1 carrot, chopped

1 stalk celery, chopped

2 cloves garlic, minced

2 tablespoons extra-virgin olive oil

2 pinches ground nutmeg

3 cans (15 ounces each) no-fat, low-sodium chicken broth

1/2 cup ditalini noodles

A handful chopped fresh parsley

Preheat oven to 375°F or a nonstick skillet to medium/medium-high heat.

Combine meat, egg, bread crumbs, cheese, garlic powder, the minced onion, salt, and pepper. Form 1/2-inch mini meatballs and place on a nonstick cookie sheet or drop into preheated nonstick skillet and cover pan with loose foil. Bake or cook on the stovetop for 12 minutes to brown balls. If you are using stovetop method, give the pan a shake every now and then to rotate the balls and brown them evenly.

While meatballs are cooking, sauté chopped carrot, celery, onion, and garlic in olive oil over medium heat in a soup pot or deep frying pan. Sprinkle vegetables with nutmeg, salt, and pepper. Cook 5 minutes. Add broth and turn heat up to high. When broth boils, drop in ditalini. Reduce heat to simmer. Cook 8 to 10 minutes, until pasta is al dente. Drop in meatballs and parsley and serve with crusty bread and a salad.

Pasta e Fagioli

3 cloves garlic, minced

2 tablespoons extra-virgin olive oil (two times around the pot)

1 carrot, peeled and finely chopped

1 medium yellow-skinned onion, peeled and chopped

2 stalks celery, from the heart (tender pieces), chopped

2 stems fresh rosemary, left whole

Several sprigs of fresh thyme, leaves stripped from stems and chopped, about 2 to 3 tablespoons

Coarse salt and black pepper, to taste

3 cans (15 ounces each) no-fat, low-sodium chicken broth

1 can (15 ounces) cannellini beans

1 cup ditalini noodles

Grated Parmigiano Reggiano or Romano cheese

Heat garlic in olive oil over medium heat in a deep pot. Add vegetables, rosemary stems, chopped thyme, and a little salt and black pepper. Cover and cook 5 minutes, stirring occasionally. Add broth and bring to a boil. Add beans and ditalini. Reduce heat to a simmer and cook 10 minutes, until noodles are al dente.

Serve immediately with a generous amount of cheese and crusty bread.
Feeds up to 4.

Quick Chick and Noodle

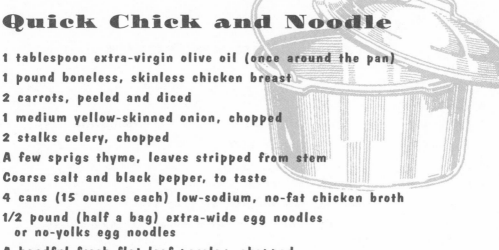

1 tablespoon extra-virgin olive oil (once around the pan)

1 pound boneless, skinless chicken breast

2 carrots, peeled and diced

1 medium yellow-skinned onion, chopped

2 stalks celery, chopped

A few sprigs thyme, leaves stripped from stem

Coarse salt and black pepper, to taste

4 cans (15 ounces each) low-sodium, no-fat chicken broth

1/2 pound (half a bag) extra-wide egg noodles
   or no-yolks egg noodles

A handful fresh flat-leaf parsley, chopped

> **Doctors** cannot say why, but many agree that chicken noodle soup, in combination with rest, is the only known cure for the common cold.

Heat olive oil over medium-high heat in a deep pot. Dice chicken breasts and add to the pot. Brown chicken. Add vegetables, thyme, and a little salt and pepper. Reduce heat to medium and cover. Sweat the vegetables for 5 minutes, stirring occasionally. Add broth. Bring to a boil. Add noodles and cook 10 minutes, or until noodles are just tender. Throw in parsley and serve immediately.

Feeds up to 6.

If you are not going to eat a whole pot in one sitting, cook noodles separately and add half a cup to each bowl of soup as you eat through the pot.

Minestra:
Greens and Beans Soup

3 heads escarole

4 cloves garlic, minced

3 tablespoons extra-virgin olive oil (three times around the pan)

Coarse salt and black pepper, to taste

3 pinches ground nutmeg

1 can (15 ounces) cannellini beans, drained

1 can (15 ounces) no-fat, low-sodium, chicken broth

**Grated fresh Parmigiano Reggiano or Romano cheese and crusty
  bread for the table**

Cut each head of escarole into quarters, working from one end to the other, resulting in leafy chunks. Place one head at a time into a colander and rinse throughly. Place pieces across layers of paper towels to dry greens. Repeat.

In a deep pot over medium heat, warm garlic in oil until it speaks by beginning to sizzle. Add greens and turn in oil until they wilt. Season with salt, pepper, and nutmeg. Add beans and broth. Simmer 10 to 15 minutes and serve with crusty bread and shaved grating cheese. Feeds 4 as a simple supper.

Leftovers are a wonderful thing; make a whole batch even for you alone. There are no words for how good this dish will make you feel — safe, warm, and happy can only begin to describe it.

Minestrone: BIG Beans and Greens Soup

1 cup ditalini noodles, cooked until al dente

3 cloves garlic, minced

2 tablespoons extra-virgin olive oil (twice around the pan)

1 small yellow onion, peeled and chopped

2 carrots, peeled and diced

2 stalks celery, from the heart, chopped

1 can (15 ounces) Roman beans, drained (Look in the Spanish or Italian foods section.) or 1 can (15 ounces) red kidney beans, drained

1 can (15 ounces) garbanzo beans, drained

1/4 pound fresh green beans, cut into thirds

1 bunch dandelion greens, about 1 pound, stems trimmed and cut into 2-inch pieces

1 can (15 ounces) diced tomatoes, drained

Coarse salt and black pepper, to taste

3 pinches ground nutmeg

4 cans (14 ounces each) no-fat, low-sodium chicken broth

Lots of grated fresh Parmigiano Reggiano or Romano cheese and crusty bread, for the table

Cook ditalini separately as you work on the soup. Drain, rinse, and toss ditalini with a touch of olive oil to prevent sticking when the noodles are cooked until al dente, about 10 minutes.

Heat garlic in olive oil over medium heat. When it speaks, add the onion, carrot, and celery. Sweat vegetables for 5 minutes. Add all other ingredients except ditalini and cheese. Bring soup to a boil, reduce heat, and simmer until greens are no longer bitter and green beans are tender, 10 to 15 minutes. Place half a cup — a good scoop of noodles — into a shallow bowl. Cover with 1 or 2 cups of hot soup. Sprinkle generously with grated cheese and serve with crusty bread for sopping up the liquid.

Makes 6 bowls. Store the noodles and soup separately to keep noodles firm.

Stracciatelle: Italian Egg Drop Soup

Literally, rag soup — Italian egg drop soup can be made in minutes and is a wonderful, healthy, late-night supper — this recipe is a favorite of all of my workaholic constituents.

For every two bowls . . .

2 cans (14 ounces each) no-fat, low-sodium chicken broth
2 eggs
3 tablespoons (a handful) grated Parmigiano Reggiano cheese
A pinch ground nutmeg
Black pepper, to taste
A handful chopped fresh flat-leaf parsley

Crusty bread

Heat broth over medium-high heat. Scramble eggs with cheese, nutmeg, and black pepper. As broth comes to a boil, drop broth to a simmer and drizzle the eggs into pot in a slow stream by scooping eggs into broth with a fork. Drizzle the eggs in a circular motion, moving slowly. The result will be rags of egg in the broth. When the eggs are all incorporated in broth, add the parsley and turn off heat. Ladle out soup and serve with crusty bread.

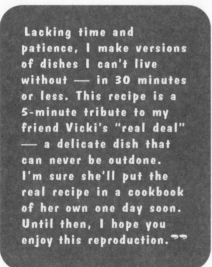

 Lacking time and patience, I make versions of dishes I can't live without — in 30 minutes or less. This recipe is a 5-minute tribute to my friend Vicki's "real deal" — a delicate dish that can never be outdone. I'm sure she'll put the real recipe in a cookbook of her own one day soon. Until then, I hope you enjoy this reproduction.

My Sister Ria's Lazy Chicken, or My Lazy Sister Ria's Chicken

Balsamic vinegar

1 1/2 pounds boneless, skinless chicken breast cutlets
(thinly sliced or pounded breast meat)

2 tablespoons extra-virgin olive oil

2 medium white-skinned potatoes, thinly sliced

1 medium white onion, halved, then thinly sliced

Montreal Steak Seasoning by McCormick (found on spice aisle), or
coarse salt and black pepper, to taste

1/2 cup (a couple glugs) white wine or chicken broth

1 small zucchini, thinly sliced

1 can (28 ounces) crushed tomatoes

10 leaves fresh basil, torn or coarsely chopped

2 sprigs fresh oregano, leaves stripped from stem and chopped

1/2 to 2/3 cup shredded Italian cheese of your choice
(provolone, mozzarella, asiago)

Rub a little splash of balsamic vinegar into each chicken breast. Heat 1 table-spoon olive oil (once around the pan) in a deep skillet over medium-high heat. Brown chicken for 2 minutes on each side. Remove chicken.

Add 1 tablespoon olive oil (once around the pan). Add a layer of thin-sliced pota-toes and onion. Sprinkle the potatoes and onion with Montreal Seasoning or coarse salt and black pepper. Let potatoes and onions cook, turning occasionally but maintaining a thin layer, until they begin to brown all over. Add a little broth or wine to pan. Spread a thin layer of zucchini across the pan on top of the pota-toes and onion and sprinkle with a touch more Montreal Seasoning or coarse salt and pepper. Top with a layer of chicken breast. Dump the crushed tomatoes even-ly over the top. Sprinkle with chopped herbs. Cover and cook until chicken is cooked through and potatoes are tender, 10 to 12 minutes.

Sprinkle the pan with the shredded Italian cheeses. Place pan under the broiler for a minute until cheese melts and begins to brown. Serve directly from the hot pan at the table. Feeds up to 6 with crusty bread.

My Friend Frank's Favorite Chicken

2 teaspoons balsamic vinegar
4 pieces boneless, skinless chicken breasts
Extra-virgin olive oil
1 large bulb fennel, halved, then thinly sliced
1 medium Spanish onion, sliced into strips, lengthwise
A handful golden raisins (about 1/4 cup packed)
1 can (14 ounces) no-fat, low-sodium chicken broth
A handful chopped fresh flat-leaf parsley
Kosher salt and cracked black pepper, to taste
Toasted pignoli (pine nuts) to garnish

Rub the balsamic vinegar into the chicken to tenderize it.

Heat a large skillet over medium-high heat. Go twice around the pan with olive oil. Cook chicken breasts 5 minutes on each side and remove from pan. Add fennel and onion. Cook, shaking pan every so often, until onion begins to caramelize (sweeten or turn caramel-golden in color), about 5 minutes. Return chicken to pan. Add raisins, broth, parsley, and salt and pepper. Heat through. Pour dish out onto a serving platter and garnish with toasted pignoli (pine nuts).

Serves 4 with crusty bread and a salad.

TEX-MEX ONE POTS

Quick Chili Con Carne . . . on the Tex Side

1 1/2 pounds lean ground beef

1 tablespoon extra-virgin olive oil (once around the pan)

1/2 medium yellow-skinned onion, chopped

4 cloves garlic, minced

1/2 bottle beer (Alcohol burns off, or use 1/2 bottle nonalcoholic beer, or twice the amount of broth.)

1/2 cup canned no-fat, low-sodium beef broth

1 can (14 ounces) crushed tomatoes

2 to 3 tablespoons chili powder (a palmful plus half again if you like it extra spicy)

1 to 1 1/2 tablespoons ground cumin (half as much as chili powder)

4 good shakes Red Hot or Tabasco sauce (liquid cayenne pepper sauce)

Kosher salt, to taste

Toppings:

Crushed tortilla chips

Chopped onion

Chopped fresh cilantro

In a deep frying pan or saucepan, brown ground beef in olive oil over medium-high heat. Add onion and garlic. Cook until the onion is translucent, about 5 minutes.

Add beer, broth, tomatoes, seasonings, and salt. Bring to a boil, then take heat down to low and simmer until ready to serve. Top with raw, chopped onion and cilantro. Serve with chips to dip, or crushed chips to top and a side of refried beans. Serves 4. Leftovers only get better. Make a whole batch, even for 1 person.

Quick Chili Con Carne . . . on the Mex Side

Substitute 1 1/2 pounds diced sirloin or strip steak for ground meat and follow same method.

Chili Con Queso

To previous recipe for ground beef chili, add 1 can (14 ounces) nacho cheese sauce, or prepare following recipe and fold in.

1 clove garlic, minced

1 small can (approximately 4 ounces) sliced jalapeños, drained (about 1/4 cup yield)

1 tablespoon extra-virgin olive oil

1 tablespoon flour

1/2 cup milk

1/2 cup shredded cheddar cheese or Mexican cheese blend

"This also makes a great party dip or Sunday game hang-out food."

Sauté garlic and jalapeño slices in olive oil over medium heat. Add flour. Stir in milk. When the mixture thickens, after 1 or 2 minutes, sprinkle in cheese. Fold into chili and follow serving instructions above.

Cajun Chili

1 1/2 pounds lean ground pork
1 tablespoon Mexican chili powder
1 tablespoon (half a palmful) ground cumin
4 shakes cayenne pepper sauce
1/2 medium yellow-skinned onion, chopped
2 cloves garlic, minced
1 stalk celery, chopped
1/2 red bell pepper, chopped
1/2 green bell pepper, chopped
1/2 bottle of beer
1 can (14 ounces) crushed tomatoes
A handful chopped fresh cilantro, optional
Kosher salt, to taste

Green Onion Corn Cakes:
1 package Jiffy corn bread mix
2 green onions, chopped

> "A spicy pork chili served up in bowls and topped with corn cakes — a Cajun not-pot-pie."

Follow directions on box for corn cakes, not corn bread. When batter is prepared, stir in chopped green onions. Bake according to package directions.

Heat a pot over high heat and a skillet or griddle with a nonstick surface over medium-high heat.

Dump the ground pork into the pot. Season with chili powder, cumin, and cayenne sauce and brown for 5 minutes. Add the onion, garlic, celery, and bell peppers and cook, giving the pan a shake now and then, for another 3 or 4 minutes.

While the chili is cooking, rub the griddle with a little butter and wipe off excess with paper towel. Make up to 4-inch corn and green-onion cakes and keep finished cakes on a plate in a warm oven until chili is done.

Back to the chili. Add beer and stir up the bits from the bottom of the pot. Stir in the tomatoes and cilantro. Bring to a boil and season with salt, to taste.

Serve the chili up in bowls and top with green onion corn cakes — with extra cakes on the side. Feeds up to 6 with a chunked vegetable salad.

White Lightning Chili

1 tablespoon extra-virgin olive oil (once around the pan)

2 pounds ground turkey breast

1 large yellow-skinned Spanish onion, chopped

1 serrano or jalapeño pepper, seeded and minced

2 cloves garlic, minced

2 tablespoons ground cumin (a palmful)

A couple shakes cayenne pepper sauce (Tabasco, Red Hot, etc.)

A palmful chopped fresh cilantro

2 cans (14 ounces each) no-fat low-sodium chicken broth

1 can (15 ounces) Great Northern/white kidney beans, drained

Coarse salt, to taste

Crushed tortilla chips for topping

Heat oil in deep skillet or pot over medium-high heat. Add turkey and cook for a couple of minutes, keeping the ground meat moving. Add onion, minced hot pepper, garlic, seasonings, and cilantro. Reduce heat to medium and cook together for 5 minutes to soften and sweeten onion. Add broth and beans. Add salt to taste. Bring to a boil. Reduce heat and simmer until you're ready to serve.

Top bowls of chili with crushed tortillas — a great thing to do with those crumbs at the end of every bag. To really jazz it up, melt shredded Monterey Jack, pepper Jack, or smoked cheddar over the top of each bowl and garnish with chips, chopped green onions, and diced yellow tomatoes. Feeds up to 6.

Who Ya Callin' Chicken? Chunky Chicken White Chili

Substitute 2 pounds of diced boneless, skinless chicken breasts for ground turkey breast and follow same method.

Three-Bean Chili

1 tablespoon extra-virgin olive oil (once around the pan)

1 serrano or jalapeño pepper, seeded and minced

1 red bell pepper, seeded and chopped

1 medium yellow-skinned onion, peeled and chopped

2 cloves garlic, minced

1 can (14 ounces) refried beans or vegetarian refried beans, used as the thickening agent

1 can (14 ounces) black beans

1 can (14 ounces) red kidney beans

1 can (28 ounces) chunky crushed tomatoes

1/2 bottle beer or 1 cup vegetable broth

6 shakes cayenne pepper sauce (Tabasco, Red Hot, etc.)

1 palmful dark chili powder (about 2 tablespoons)

1/2 palmful ground cumin (about 1 tablespoon)

A handful fresh cilantro leaves, chopped

Coarse salt, to taste

Toppings:

4 green onions, chopped

Chopped red and yellow tomatoes

Diced avocados

Crushed tortilla chips

Grated pepper Jack cheese or smoked cheddar

Heat olive oil over medium heat in a deep pot. Add peppers, onion, and garlic and cook for 5 minutes to soften and sweeten vegetables. Add all other ingredients. Bring chili to a boil, reduce heat to low, and simmer until ready to serve or for at least 10 minutes to combine flavors.

Serve with any combination of toppings from suggested list, or create your own concoctions. Makes 6 bowls. Left-overs get better — make a big batch even to feed 1.

Sorta Posole: Pork and Corn Stew

This recipe uses lean and tender cuts of pork so that the stew does not require more than 30 minutes of preparation time. "Sorta" is not a person or place — it is Sort of Posole. If your market does sell canned hominy, substitute it in the same amounts as the corn and your dish will be all the more authentic.

Extra-virgin olive oil

1 1/2 pounds boneless pork loin chops, diced

1 medium Spanish onion, chopped

1 fresh serrano or jalapeño pepper, finely chopped

3 cloves garlic, finely chopped

1 palmful ground cumin, about 2 tablespoons

Kosher salt and cracked black pepper to taste

10 to 12 tomatillos, husked

1/2 fresh lime

2 to 3 stems fresh oregano, leaves stripped and chopped

4 to 6 stems of fresh thyme, leaves stripped and chopped

2 cans (14 ounces each) no-fat, low-sodium chicken broth

2 cans white-kernel corn, drained, or 3 ears fresh corn, scraped from the cob

"Posole is the Spanish word for hominy, which looks like large-kernel corn. It can also refer to a pork stew, the recipe for which calls for several cups of the jumbo kernels."

Toppings:
- ☐ Salsas
- ☐ Croutons
- ☐ Olives
- ☐ Onions
- ☐ Herbed garlic toasts or broken tortilla chip pieces

In a large, heavy pot, coated lightly with olive oil (twice around the pan), brown the pork over medium-high heat. When the pork is brown, after 5 or 6 minutes, add onion, serrano or jalapeño pepper, and garlic. Reduce heat to medium and let it hang out another 5 or 6 minutes, until the onions becomes translucent. Add cumin and salt and pepper.

While the pork and onion are cooking, process the tomatillos, the juice of the 1/2 lime, and the oregano and thyme leaves in a food processor until it has reached a salsa-like consistency. Dump this into the stewpot and cook the tomatillos for 2 or 3 minutes before adding the next ingredients. (Cooking the tomatillos mellows their bitter taste.)

**In the United States, we know ground hominy as grits. In the South, it's easy to find canned hominy kernels. In the North, the canned product is hard to spot. You can buy dried posole at specialty stores, but it needs to be soaked and slow-cooked before use. Canned hominy tastes a little like white corn. So, for time's sake, we substitute corn fresh off the cob or canned white corn in our Sorta Posole.

Stir in the chicken broth and the drained corn. Heat stew through. Serve with toppings of your choice. This is a complete meal on its own — but if you want to add a salad, try chunked tomato, onion, and avocado with the juice of the remaining 1/2 lime and a drizzle of olive oil. Serves up to 4.

Sundance Beef Pot Pies

2 teaspoons (a couple of real good shakes) each ground cumin and chili powder

4 shakes Red Hot, or other liquid cayenne pepper sauce

1 1/2 pounds beef-tip steak, thinly sliced

1 box Jiffy corn bread mix (for which you will need 1 egg and a little milk to mix)

2 tablespoons extra-virgin olive oil (twice around the pan)

1 red bell pepper, seeded and chopped

1 medium yellow-skinned Spanish onion, peeled and chopped

1 small can (14 ounces) diced tomatoes

1/2 bunch fresh thyme, leaves stripped from stems and chopped

2 tablespoons butter

Rub the cumin, chili powder, and Red Hot into the steak.

Preheat oven to 375° F. Prepare Jiffy mix according to directions on box. Spoon the mix onto a greased cookie sheet in six 4-inch rounds — you are making corn bread lids for your soup bowls. Place in oven and bake until golden brown, about 10 to 12 minutes.

> **No affiliation to Robert Redford, his companies, or his former on-screen roles . . . unfortunately.**

Heat a big nonstick skillet till hot. Cook steak 3 minutes on one side, 2 minutes on the other. Remove from heat and let rest.

Reduce heat to medium-high. Go twice around the pan with oil. Sauté the bell pepper and onion for 5 minutes, until onion begins to color around edges. Dump in the tomatoes and a palmful of the chopped thyme. Cut steak into bite-size pieces and drop into pan. Drop heat to low.

Take remaining thyme leaves and place them in a small bowl with butter. Microwave butter and thyme on high for 20 seconds. Brush the corn tops with thyme butter. Scoop beef mixture into bowls and top each bowl with a corn-crusted top. Serves 4.

PUT A LID ON IT:

Quick Bread "Lids" for Chilis and Stews

☐ Bacon, browned and chopped

☐ Fresh chives

☐ Chopped green onions

☐ Cheddar cheese and chopped jalapeños

☐ A few kernels canned or frozen corn and a pinch or two cayenne pepper

☐ Fresh thyme and black pepper

As in Sundance Beef Pot Pie recipe, corn muffin tops are a delicious and clever topper for any of the chilis and Tex-Mex one pots listed in this section, creating 30-minute pot pies. For each box of Jiffy corn muffin mix, your yield should be 6 tops. Try adding any of the above to the batter to flavor the toppers and better complement your meal.

CONTINENTAL FAVORITES

Chicken and Dumplings

2 boneless, skinless chicken breasts, 4 pieces, up to 2 pounds

1/2 cup all-purpose flour

Coarse salt and white or black pepper, to taste (White is nice with this, if you have it.)

2 tablespoons extra-virgin olive oil (once around the pan)

2 stalks celery, trimmed, sliced down the center lengthwise, then chopped into small cubes

1 medium white onion, chopped

1 white potato, peeled and diced

2 carrots, peeled and diced

1 box Jiffy biscuit mix, prepared according to directions on box

A handful fresh flat-leaf parsley, chopped

3 cans (14 ounces each) low-sodium, no-fat chicken broth

1 cup water

Cut chicken into big chunks. Spill a handful or two of flour onto a shallow dish. Salt and pepper the flour. Coat the chicken chunks by tossing them all through the flour and rolling them around a bit. Discard the extra flour and wash hands.

To give the dumplings room to cook, divide your ingredients and cook in 2 separate pans. Heat a little oil in each of 2 skillets or frying pans over medium-high heat. Place chicken pieces in hot pans and brown for 4 minutes on each side. Remove chicken from pans and reduce heat to medium. Add chopped veggies and sauté for 2 or 3 minutes, giving the pans a shake now and then.

While veggies cook, mix up 1 box of Jiffy biscuit mix, adding a handful of parsley to the batter. Add 1 1/2 cans chicken broth and 1/2 cup water to each pan. Add chicken back to pots. Bring liquids to a boil. Drop in biscuit mix a heaping tablespoon at a time, 5 or 6 dumplings per pan. Cover with foil or lids and simmer 8 to 10 minutes. Uncover and cook an additional 3 to 5 minutes or until sauce thickens to desired consistency. Adjust salt and pepper to your taste.

Feeds up to 6 with a green salad. Leftovers only get better tasting — don't be afraid of making a whole batch even if you live alone.

Quick Coq au Vin

2 full chicken breasts, 4 pieces breast, total, about 1 1/2 pounds

3 chicken thighs (Ask the butcher to bone and skin it for you.)

1/2 cup all-purpose flour (a couple handfuls)

Coarse salt and cracked black pepper, to taste

1/3 cup extra-virgin olive oil (4 or 5 times around the pan)

1/2 pound mushrooms, sliced (Many produce departments sell packages of pre-sliced, ready-to-use mushrooms.)

1 medium Spanish onion, halved and thinly sliced lengthwise

2 cloves garlic, minced

1 1/2 cups good, dry, red wine

1 can (14 ounces) no-fat chicken broth

1/2 bunch fresh thyme, leaves stripped from stem and chopped (yield about 3 tablespoons)

3 to 4 tablespoons tomato paste

Giant Garlic Croutons:

1 baguette (long, crusty, French bread), cut into 2-inch thick rounds

1/4 cup extra-virgin olive oil

1 clove garlic, peeled and coarsely chopped

Cut breasts and thighs into large chunks. Mix flour with salt and pepper on a plate. Dust the pieces of chicken with the seasoned flour. Heat some olive oil in a large skillet over medium-high heat. Brown and crisp the chicken pieces by cooking for 4 to 5 minutes on each side. Remove the chicken. Add the mushrooms, onion, and garlic to pan. Give the pan a shake every minute or so. Cook onions and mushrooms down for 5 minutes. Add red wine. Scrape up all the good bits of gunk off the bottom of the pan. Add chicken broth. Return chicken to pan. Sprinkle pan with a generous amount of fresh thyme. Bring to a boil. Stir in tomato paste. Reduce heat to medium low and let simmer until broth begins to thicken, about 10 minutes.

While chicken finishes cooking, broil completely dry, bread rounds on cookie sheet. Evenly brown the bread rounds on both sides. Remove from oven. In a small dish or bowl, microwave the olive oil and garlic for 30 seconds on high. If, like me, you don't use or have a microwave, place the dish in a hot oven for a minute or two. Heating the oil infuses the flavor of the garlic into it. Brush the oil over the toasted French bread round.

To serve, set the garlic croutons in the juice and all around the edge of the skillet of chicken. Bring the whole pan right to the table and serve it right from the hot pot. Makes 4 to 6 servings — leftovers freeze well and improve in flavor.

Four-Season Burgundy Beef

1 package (16 ounces) extra-wide egg noodles

2 pats butter (a couple of thin slices off the stick)

A handful chopped fresh flat-leaf parsley

2 pounds beef fillet tips or tender sirloin, cut into bite-size cubes

A couple handfuls all-purpose flour

Coarse salt and black pepper, to taste

Extra-virgin olive oil (twice around the pan, about 2 tablespoons)

2 medium white onions, peeled and chopped

12 to 16 firm, small mushroom caps, halved

2 cloves garlic, minced

1 1/2 cups good burgundy wine

3 to 4 sprigs of fresh thyme, leaves stripped from stems, chopped

1 bay leaf

1 can (14 ounces) no-fat beef broth (Keep an extra can on hand to reheat any leftovers with.)

2 to 3 tablespoons tomato paste

Start a pot of water to boil for egg noodles. When the boil is rapid, cook noodles until al dente (this means still slightly firm to the bite — not too mushy). When they are ready, stop whatever you are doing. Drain the noodles and cold-shock them under running water for a few seconds to stop the cooking process. Drain them well and place them back in the still hot pot. Toss with butter and parsley and let them hang out until beef is done.

Pat the beef cubes with paper towels. Spill a couple of handfuls all-purpose flour onto a shallow dish. Season the flour with salt and pepper. Toss the cubes a few at a time, gently coating with flour. Place floured cubes on a separate plate to prevent some cubes from getting too gooey and gopped up.

When all the cubes are lightly coated, heat olive oil in a deep skillet over medium-high heat. Add beef and sauté the cubes 6 to 8 minutes, turning once, until browned. Remove meat from pot and dump in onions, mushrooms, and garlic. Cook veggies down, giving the pan a shake every now and then, for 5 minutes, or until mushrooms begin to brown and onions begin to soften. Add wine and scrape up all the good bits of gunk from the bottom. Add thyme, bay leaf, broth, and beef. Stir in tomato paste and simmer another 5 to 10 minutes to thicken sauce a little. Remove bay leaf. Serve scoops of the beef and burgundy over beds of parsleyed egg noodles.

Feeds 4 well, with crusty bread and a simple salad of greens dressed with lemon juice, olive oil, salt, and pepper. Again, the leftovers only get better. Make a whole batch even for 1 or 2.

Beef and Cider Pot

2 tablespoons extra-virgin olive oil (twice around the pan)

1 1/2 pounds beef sirloin, cut into bite-size cubes

Worcestershire sauce

Montreal Steak Seasoning by McCormick, or coarse salt and black pepper, to taste

2 medium white-skinned potatoes, thinly sliced

1 medium yellow-skinned onion, chopped

2 carrots, peeled and diced

1 turnip, peeled and diced

4 tablespoons all-purpose flour (a couple handfuls)

1 1/2 cups apple cider

1 tablespoon cider vinegar, or white vinegar

A handful chopped fresh flat-leaf parsley

1 cup shredded cheddar, or smoked cheddar cheese

Pour 1 tablespoon olive oil in the bottom of a deep, heavy skillet and heat over high heat. Add beef cubes to pot and brown for 3 to 5 minutes. Sprinkle with Worcestershire sauce and Montreal Seasoning or salt and pepper. Remove the meat and reduce heat a little, to medium high.

Add another tablespoon of olive oil. Cover the bottom of the skillet with a layer of thinly sliced potatoes. Sprinkle with Montreal Seasoning or salt and black pepper. Brown the potatoes for 3 or 4 minutes on each side and remove. Add onion, carrot, and turnip bits. Cook for 5 minutes. Sprinkle with a couple of handfuls flour and cook another minute. Add cider, vinegar, parsley, and beef cubes to pot. Combine ingredients well.

Rest the sliced potatoes across the top of skillet and cover with lid or foil. Reduce heat to low and simmer for a last few minutes, until veggies are all just tender. Uncover your dish and sprinkle the potatoes with cheddar or smoked cheddar. Place skillet under broiler to melt and brown cheese. Serve from the pot.

Feeds 4, well. This dish makes great tailgate party food or a pot luck supper contribution.

Quick Cassoulet

2 chicken thighs (Ask the butcher to bone and skin them.)

2 pieces boneless, skinless chicken breast (1 breast, about 3/4 pound)

2 tablespoons extra-virgin olive oil (twice around the pan)

4 sweet sausages

1 carrot, peeled and diced

1 stalk celery, diced

1 small onion, peeled and chopped

2 cloves garlic, minced

1/2 cup (a couple of glugs) dry white wine

1 can (15 ounces) cannellini beans (white beans)

6 to 8 sprigs fresh thyme, leaves stripped from stem and chopped

1 bay leaf

Salt and freshly ground pepper to taste

1 can (14 ounces) diced tomatoes

1 can (14 ounces) no-fat, low-sodium chicken broth

Giant Garlic Croutons:

1 baguette (long, crusty, French bread), cut into 2-inch thick rounds

1/4 cup extra-virgin olive oil

1 clove garlic

Dice chicken into bite-size pieces. Heat a deep pot or skillet over medium-high heat. Add 1 tablespoon olive oil (once around the pan) and whole sausages and diced chicken to pot. Brown for 5 minutes. Remove sausages and chicken; set aside. Add a second tablespoon of olive oil. Cook carrot, celery, and onion for 5 minutes, frequently giving the pot a good shake. Add garlic. Douse pan with wine and scrape up all the good bits of gunk. Add beans, thyme, bay leaf, salt and pepper, tomatoes, and broth. Slice sausages into bite-size pieces and return sausages and chicken to pan to finish cooking. Bring dish to a boil, reduce heat to low, and simmer 10 minutes. Discard bay leaf.

To make croutons, broil bread rounds, completely dry, on cookie sheet. Evenly brown the bread rounds on both sides. Remove from oven. In a small dish or bowl, microwave the olive oil and garlic for 30 seconds on high. If, like me, you don't use or have a microwave, place the dish in a hot oven for a minute or two. Heating the oil infuses the flavor of the garlic into it. Brush the oil over the toasted French bread rounds.

To serve, set the garlic croutons into the juice and all around the edge of the skillet of cassoulet. Bring the whole pan right to the table or counter and serve it right from the hot pot. Feeds 4, well — improves with age, so make a whole pot for 1 or 2 as well.

Pork Chops and Homemade Chunky Applesauce

6 boneless pork chops, 3/4-inch thick
Balsamic vinegar
Black pepper
1 tablespoon extra-virgin olive oil (once around the pan)
6 sprigs fresh thyme, leaves stripped from stems and chopped

2 feet aluminum foil, folded in half, then in half again

Homemade Chunky Applesauce:
8 Macintosh apples, peeled, cored, and cut into chunks
1 cup (a small bottleful) all-natural/organic apple juice or cider
A couple pinches ground cinnamon
A palmful brown sugar
A pinch ground ginger
A pinch ground nutmeg

Rub chops with a little balsamic vinager to tenderize. Heat olive oil in a deep skillet over medium-high heat. (Chops should sizzle when placed in pan.) Cook chops 5 or 6 minutes. Turn and season chops with pepper and thyme. Place an aluminum foil tent on top of the chops, reduce heat to medium, and cook another 6 minutes. Then remove from heat and let stand until ready to serve, allowing juices to distribute.

While chops cook, cook the apple chunks over medium-high heat with the apple juice. As the juice boils, stir and mush the apples a bit as they cook down. (You want to leave the sauce chunky when you use nice fresh apples.) Sprinkle the sauce with cinnamon, sugar, ginger, and nutmeg. Reduce heat and simmer until sauce thickens, about 7 to 10 minutes.

These chops and sauce are delicious paired with Spinach with Garlic and Nutmeg (page 70). Serves 6.

Twilight Time Turkey Patties and Cranberry Sauce

1 handful pecan pieces (sold in bulk in candy and nuts section of market)

1 cup instant mashed potato flakes

1 1/3 pounds ground turkey breast

1 small white onion, grated

1 handful chopped fresh flat-leaf parsley

2 sprigs fresh thyme, stripped from stems and chopped

2 tablespoons extra-virgin olive oil (twice around the pan)

1 teaspoon poultry seasoning

Salt and black pepper, to taste

1 can (16 ounces) whole berry cranberry sauce

Grind pecans in processor or place in baggie and whack with a blunt instrument. Mix pecans with instant potato flakes in a shallow dish. Place turkey in a bowl and grate the onion over and into same bowl with a handheld grater. Combine with parsley, thyme, poultry seasoning, and salt and pepper. Form into 6 patties. Heat oil in a nonstick skillet over medium-high heat. Coat patties in potato-and-nut mixture. Cook patties for 5 minutes on each side.

Serve with plenty of cranberry sauce. Feeds 4 to 6 with a green salad, and bread and butter.

Goodness Gracious, That's Great Goulash!

1 pound elbow macaroni, cooked according to directions on box

2 pounds lean ground beef

1 medium white onion, chopped

2 cloves garlic, minced

1 teaspoon ground cumin (a few healthy pinches)

1 tablespoon (half a palmful) paprika

A pinch ground nutmeg

Salt and pepper, to taste

2 sprigs fresh marjoram, chopped, or a healthy sprinkle of dried

1 can (14 ounces) crushed tomatoes

3 rounded tablespoons sour cream

2 pats butter or a drizzle of extra-virgin olive oil

Chopped fresh parsley

1 teaspoon caraway seeds (Pour a little into the center of your palm and eyeball it.)

While the macaroni is cooking, heat a deep skillet over medium-high heat. Add ground beef and brown. Grate an onion into the pot with a hand grater. Add garlic and seasonings. Mix in tomatoes. Heat through, then stir in sour cream. Drain macaroni and toss with butter or oil, parsley, and caraway seeds.

Serve scoops of goulash over bowls of macaroni. Feeds up to 6 — go for leftovers if you are fewer in number — and freezes well.

Big-Belly Beef Stew

3 tablespoons extra-virgin olive oil (3 times around the pan)

2 pounds tender sirloin, cut into bite-size cubes

4 to 6 small white-skinned potatoes, chunked

2 medium white onions, peeled and chopped

3 cloves garlic, minced

1 can (14 ounces) no-fat beef broth

1 can water, fill up the empty beef broth can

2 bay leaves

3 tablespoons tomato paste

2 pinches ground cinnamon

Coarse salt and black pepper, to taste

A few tablespoons red wine vinegar

A handful chopped fresh flat-leaf parsley

Heat oil in deep skillet over high heat. Brown beef cubes for 5 minutes, giving the pan a shake now and then. Remove beef. Add potatoes and reduce heat to medium. Cook potatoes for a few minutes. Dump in onions and garlic. Add broth and lift up all the gunk. Add water, bay leaves, tomato paste, cinnamon, and salt and pepper. Return beef to pan. Bring to a boil. Allow mixture to cook until potatoes are tender and sauce has reduced some, about 10 minutes. Turn off heat and let stand 5 minutes. Discard bay leaves. Stir in vinegar and parsley and serve warm or at room temperature with crusty bread.

Feeds a family of up to 6.

Dan's Favorite Shrimp and Scallop Creole

2 cups water
1 cup enriched white rice

1/2 andouille or chorizo smoked sausage, diced
2 stalks celery, diced
1 medium yellow-skinned onion, peeled and chopped
1 green bell pepper, seeded and diced
2 cloves garlic, minced
1 can (14 ounces) no-fat, low-sodium chicken broth
1 can (28 ounces) chunky style crushed or diced tomatoes
1 can (15 ounces) crushed tomatoes
1 teaspoon each chili powder and ground cumin (1/4 palmful of each)
6 shakes cayenne pepper sauce
Black pepper, to taste
1 bay leaf
6 sprigs fresh thyme, leaves stripped from stems and chopped
1 tablespoon extra-virgin olive oil
12 to 16 large sea scallops (purchased no more than 1 day in advance)
12 to 16 jumbo shrimp, cooked, cleaned and, deveined
4 green onions, thinly sliced

Boil water, then add rice. Reduce heat to simmer and cook, covered, for 15 to 20 minutes.

While rice cooks, heat deep pot over medium-high heat. Add diced sausage and brown for 3 to 5 minutes. Add celery, onion, and bell pepper. Cook vegetables down for 5 minutes more. Add garlic and give the pot a good shake. Add half the broth, all of the tomatoes, and the seasonings: chili powder and cumin, cayenne pepper sauce, black pepper, bay leaf, and thyme. Reduce heat to low and simmer Creole sauce while you cook the scallops. Discard bay leaf.

Heat olive oil in a nonstick skillet over medium to medium-high heat. Cook half the scallops at a time and cook 2 to 3 minutes on each side, or until scallops begin to caramelize on each side. When all the scallops are done, add them, with the shrimp, to the pan. Pour your Creole sauce over the seafood. Add reserved broth to loosen up the dish a bit. Turn off heat. Scoop seafood creole into bowls and sprinkle with green onions. Scoop out 1/2 cup of cooked rice and place in the center of filled soup bowls — placing the rice on top of the stew keeps it firm. Makes 4 to 6 servings, depending on the amount of seafood used.

Jambalika: Quick Jambalaya

White enriched rice

2 tablespoons extra-virgin olive oil (twice around the pan)

1 full, large, boneless, skinless chicken breast (2 pieces), cut into bite-size pieces

2 pieces boneless, skinless chicken thighs, diced

3/4 pound andouille or chorizo smoked sausage, thinly sliced on an angle, or substitute 4 links chicken andouille sausage (available in many markets)

16 cooked, peeled, deveined jumbo shrimp

The next three ingredients are referred to as the holy trinity in Cajun country:

1 celery heart, 4 or 5 small, tender stalks, chopped

1 medium yellow-skinned onion, chopped

1 green bell pepper, seeded and diced

4 cloves garlic, minced

1 can (14 ounces) no-fat, low-sodium, chicken broth

1 tablespoon (half a palmful) each ground cumin and chili powder

A few shakes cayenne pepper sauce (Tabasco or Red Hot)

1 can (28 ounces) diced tomatoes

1 bay leaf

6 to 8 sprigs fresh thyme, leaves stripped from stems and chopped

2 tablespoons gumbo filé (a powder of sassafras leaves found in the spice section), or add 1/2 pound okra, chopped (see Note)

Chopped scallions to garnish

> **"Jambalika is a trendy take on Cajun cooking."**

> **Note: Filé and okra will both thicken your jambalaya without the use of a roux, a mixture of flour and butter.**

Start a pot of plain white enriched rice, following the directions on the box for 4 to 6 servings, before you start Jambalika. The rice will take a good 20 to 30 minutes, as long as the Jambalika will take to prepare.

In a deep pot, heat 1 tablespoon olive oil (once around the pan) over medium-high heat. Brown chicken and sausage for 3 to 5 minutes. Remove meats from pot. Add a little more olive oil and the celery, onion, bell pepper, and garlic. Let veggies hang out in the pot for 3 to 5 minutes to soften and sweeten them, giving the pot a shake every now and then.

Return the chicken and andouille to the pot. When the meats are all combined with the veggies, add the broth, seasonings, tomatoes, and herbs. Bring to a boil. Drop heat to a simmer. Stir in filé powder or okra. Cook until the mixture thickens, about 3 minutes. Discard bay leaf. Serve with a scoop of rice dropped into the center of each bowlful of Jambalika; garnish with scallions. Serves up to 6.

Jambasta: Jambalaya Pasta

2 tablespoons (twice around the pan) extra-virgin olive oil

3/4 pound boneless, skinless chicken breast, diced and rubbed with:

1/2 teaspoon ground cumin

1 teaspoon chili powder

4 shakes cayenne pepper sauce

1/4 pound smoked ham, andouille, chorizo, or chicken andouille sausage, chopped

24 peeled and deveined medium shrimp

2 tablespoons all-purpose flour (2 sprinklings across the pan)

A palmful fresh thyme leaves, plus extra to garnish

2 cloves garlic, minced

1 cup no-fat, low-sodium chicken broth

1/2 cup half-and-half

3 shakes Worcestershire sauce

1 cup grated Parmigiano Reggiano cheese

1 box (14 ounces) egg fettucine, cooked until al dente

Cracked black pepper, to taste

In a large skillet or frying pan, heat oil over high heat. Add chicken and ham or sausage and cook for 5 minutes to brown. Add shrimp and cook until it whitens, only a minute or so. Sprinkle pan with flour. Cook another minute, then add the thyme and garlic. Shake the pan and add the broth, picking up all of the bits from the bottom of the pan. Stir in the half-and-half and a couple of shakes of Worcestershire sauce and 1/3 cup of Parmigiano cheese. Bring to a boil. Reduce heat and let simmer for 5 minutes.

Toss drained fettucine with sauce and remaining cheese. Top with freshly ground black pepper and extra thyme. Feeds up to 6 with a tomato and onion salad.

great
gatherings

I love to share time and food with friends, but entertaining for big groups can keep me in the kitchen all night, away from the people I invited over to visit with. The party menus I see in the pages of magazines are always beautiful, but often too complicated for my hectic schedule, especially around any holiday.

There are alternatives. Entertaining in little groups makes a big difference. Conversation is more meaningful, the laughs bigger and the work, a whole lot easier. Not overdoing it is another practical tip. Who needs mountains of leftovers that have sat at room temperature for several hours? Simple menus with short preparation times can keep it all manageable. The less you do, the better the foods will taste.

Six Big Menus for Small Cocktail Parties For cocktail parties of 8 to 12, try one of these fast, easy, and fun menus. Each can be made in very little time, allowing you to attend your own party. Cool.

Five Fabulous Meatballs Meatballs are the all-time favorite party food, so I have included five fabulous recipes for them in this chapter. A batch of any can be made in 30 minutes. Serve meatballs with cheese, olives, smoked nuts, hummus, and bread sticks, for example. And presto, party time!

If dinner parties are more your speed, copy a few of the 30-minute meals onto recipe cards. Invite three or four couples to a cooking party. Pile the raw ingredients next to a card for each couple. Have a holiday cook-off. At evening's end, everyone has contributed, had fun, and eaten well.

menu

Mini Turkey Patties with Cranberry Sauce

Chutney, Nut and Cheddar Cheese Balls with Assorted Crackers and Flat breads

Pear, Grape, Smoked Cheese, and Meat Board

Spiked Berries and French-Vanilla Parfaits

TIMING NOTE:
The cheese ball mixture takes moments to prepare, but should be chilled the day before you plan to entertain to make the mixture firm enough to shape.

Mini Turkey Patties with Cranberry Sauce

A handful pecans (2 to 3 ounces), available in bulk foods aisle of market)

1 cup instant mashed potato flakes

1 1/3 pounds ground turkey breast

1 small onion, grated or minced

1 stalk celery, finely chopped

1 teaspoon poultry seasoning

Coarse salt and black pepper, to taste

2 sprigs fresh thyme, leaves stripped from stem and chopped

3 tablespoons olive or corn oil (three times around the pan)

1 can (16 ounces) whole berry cranberry sauce

A handful chopped fresh flat-leaf parsley

Chop pecans in processor or place in baggy and whack with a blunt instrument. Mix pecans with instant potato flakes in a shallow dish.

Place turkey in a bowl and grate the onion over and into same bowl with a hand-held grater. Combine turkey and onion with celery, poultry seasoning, salt, pepper and thyme.

Heat oil in a nonstick skillet over medium heat. Form turkey into 12 to 15 small patties. As you work, coat each pattie in potato-and-nut mixture and drop them into the skillet. Cook patties until potato and nut crust is deep golden brown, about 3 to 4 minutes on each side. Serve with plenty of whole berry cranberry sauce mixed with a little fresh parsley for color. Makes 12 to 15 hors d'oeuvres.

Chutney, Nut, and Cheddar Cheese Balls

1 brick (8 ounces) cream cheese
1/4 cup butter (1/2 stick)
Fresh gingerroot (2 inches) grated
A pinch allspice
1/8 teaspoon ground nutmeg (2 pinches)
1 package (10 ounces) shredded cheddar cheese
1/2 jar (4 ounces) mango chutney, available in condiment aisle, or 1/3 cup mincemeat pie filling (available in baking aisle of market)
1 cup macadamia or cashew nuts
A handful chopped fresh flat-leaf parsley

Soften cream cheese and butter in microwave on defrost setting for 45 seconds. Dump into food processor with ginger, allspice, nutmeg, cheddar, and chutney or mincemeat. Pulse the ingredients together until combined. Scrape out of processor and into a glass bowl. Cover and chill until firm or overnight.

When you are ready to serve, chop nuts in a food processor, until coarsely ground. Dump onto a plate and mix with a little parsley. Remove cheese mixture from frige. Scoop out a heaping teaspoon of cheese mixture at a time. Shape into balls and roll in the nut and parsley mixture. Or, form all of the cheese mixture into a large ball or two medium balls and coat with nuts. Serve larger cheese balls as a spread, with assorted crackers and flat breads. Makes about 40 small balls, or 1 large ball for 12 guests.

Pear, Grape, Smoked Cheese, and Meat Board

In the specialty cheese case of your market, look for:
- ☐ Applewood, a smoked derby cheese from Great Britain
- ☐ Smoked cheddars
- ☐ Smoked provolones
- ☐ Smoked mozzarella cheeses

All should be readily available.

At the deli counter of your market, choose from:
- ☐ Smoked ham
- ☐ Smoked turkey
- ☐ Smoked chicken
- ☐ Dried sausage

Buy a half-pound chunk of 1 or 2 smoked meats to cube or slice into strips and offer with your cheese selections. Or, slice up 1 or 2 dried-sausage selections, also found near deli area.

Arrange 2 or 3 cheeses, each 1/2 to 3/4 pounds, on a cutting board. Scatter cubed meats around the board and decorate with a small selection of ripe pears and bunches of grapes.

Spiked Berries and French-Vanilla Parfaits

3 cups assorted fresh berries (raspberries, blackberries, sliced strawberries)

3 jiggers Frangelico hazelnut liqueur or Amaretto

3 teaspoons sugar

2 pints French Vanilla ice cream

Assorted cocktail glasses

Dump berries in a small serving bowl. Douse with liqueur and sprinkle with sugar. Combine and let sit until ready to serve. Layer berries with tablespoonfuls of ice cream in small cocktail glasses of different shapes for a fun, unexpected cocktail-party offering. Makes 12 parfaits.

menu

Meat Tapas with Garlic and Sherry

Warm Chili and Cheese Dip with Tri-Color Peppers and Tortilla Chips

Tomato and Garlic Bread Rounds

Assorted Olives

Sangria Slushes

Meat Tapas with Garlic and Sherry

3 tablespoons extra virgin olive oil (three times around the pan)

3 cloves garlic, peeled, coarsely sliced

3 pounds meat tenderloin, cubed into 1/2 to 1 inch pieces
   (Use beef tenderloin filet, pork tenderloin, or chicken tenders,
   or a combination totaling 3 pounds)

Coarse salt and pepper, to taste

1 cup Madeira or good Spanish sherry

A handful chopped fresh flat-leaf parsley

Bamboo or wooden skewers (8 inch) for serving

Heat oil and garlic in a heavy skillet over medium high heat. Pat meat with paper towels to dry, just before dropping into heated skillet. Cook meat for 7 or 8 minutes, until browned. Sprinkle with coarse salt and pepper. Douse pan with madeira or sherry, scraping off all the juicy bits from the bottom of pan. Reduce the liquid for 1 minute and transfer meat to a serving bowl. Sprinkle with parsley for color. Serves 12 as an appetizer.

Long bamboo skewers make great mini-spears. Put them in a small glass alongside the meats.

> "Tapas is a Spanish term describing a little dish. Tapas bars set out many little dishes that combined make up the meal. Tapas makes sharing food with friends fun and easy."

Warm Chili and Cheese Dip with Tri-Color Peppers and Tortilla Chips

1 can (15 ounces) chili with meat, no beans

1 brick (8 ounces) cream cheese or reduced-fat cream cheese

1 small can (4 ounces) sliced jalapeño peppers, drained and chopped

1 package (10 ounces) shredded cheddar or reduced-fat cheddar

A handful fresh cilantro, chopped

1 each yellow, green, and red bell peppers, seeded and cut into thin strips, lengthwise

3 bags assorted tortilla chips (10 to 12 ounces each) — blue corn, red corn, black bean, white corn, etc.

Combine chili, cream cheese, jalapeño and cheddar in saucepan and cook over medium-low heat until smooth. Stir in cilantro and transfer to fondue pot or oven-safe bowl, warmed in a 350° F oven for 10 minutes. Serves up to 12 guests.

Place a platter of tri-colored pepper strips and a basket of assorted tortilla chips next to your chili-cheese concoction for dipping.

Tomato and Garlic Bread Rounds

1 loaf crusty bread, French or Italian, about 24 inches long

3/4 cup extra-virgin olive oil

3 cloves garlic, popped from skin and left whole

2 large, ripe vine tomatoes

Cut bread into 24 slices. Place bread rounds on cookie sheet and toast in 325°F oven until lightly browned, about 7 or 8 minutes. Warm garlic and oil in microwave on high for 45 seconds or in a small saucepan over medium-low heat, until the garlic speaks. Brush rounds with garlic oil. Cut ripe tomatoes in half and rub the garlic-oil-brushed sides of the rounds against the flesh of the ripe tomatoes, rubbing six rounds with each half tomato. Serve immediately. Makes 24 rounds.

Assorted Olives

Olives are always a welcome party food, too. Whether green, black, or violet (indicating degree of ripeness) they are a healthy, delicious snack.

Try tasting different kinds. Some are slightly bitter, others more aromatic. They shouldn't be too salty, as a rule, and good olives are firm, not soft.

You can save money by buying them in bulk in your market.

Sangria Slushes

2 pints lemon ice
3 bottles of Spanish Rioja red wine

Drop a scoop or two of lemon ice into wine glasses and fill up with red wine — a simple and delicious party slush. Serves 12.

menu

Mamma Elsa's Chicken Liver Pâté

Stuffed Mushrooms with Seafood or Sweet Sausage

Hummus and Flat Breads

Cheese Board with Fresh and Dried Fruits

Smoked Almonds

TIMING NOTES:
To prepare both pâté and mushrooms in 30 minutes,
read through both recipes and acquaint yourself with them.
Start pâté, according to directions, and while it cooks,
start mushrooms.

You'll have to bob back and forth between a couple of pans
at a time. If this makes you nervous, talk your honey,
your kids, or your best friend, into being a second set of
hands the first time you decide to serve these dishes.
The rest of this menu consists of ready-to-serve packaged
products and fresh fruits that are ready to go as soon
as you transfer them to serving dishes.

Mamma Elsa's Chicken Liver Pâté

1 1/2 sticks unsalted butter

3 medium onions, sliced thin

1 pound chicken livers, washed and dried (pat with paper towels)

Coarse salt and black pepper, to taste

1/4 teaspoon (a couple of good pinches) ground thyme

2 baguettes (thin, crusty loaves of French bread), sliced at the bakery the day of the party

Melt butter in heavy-bottom pot over medium heat. Add onions and let cook until golden and soft, stirring occasionally, about 10 minutes. Add livers and cook until well done, about another 10 to 12 minutes. Sprinkle with salt, pepper, and thyme. Blend in food processor, while hot. Place in serving crocks and serve warm or cover and chill, for up three days before party. Swirl and peak the top of the crockful of pâté using the tip of a fork. Serves 8 to 10, as a party offering.

Stuffed Mushrooms with Seafood or Sweet Sausage

2 tablespoons extra-virgin olive oil (twice around the pan)

24 large, stuffing mushrooms, stems removed (save 12 stems for stuffing recipe)

4 cloves garlic, minced

1/2 cup sherry

Sausage or seafood stuffing (see following recipes)

Warm olive oil in a heavy skillet over medium heat . Add mushroom caps and cook, turning once, for 8 to 10 minutes. Add garlic. Cook another minute or two, giving the pan a couple of good shakes. Add sherry and coat mushrooms with another couple of good shakes of the pan. Stuff caps with the seafood or sausage stuffing and brown under broiler to crisp the stuffing just before serving.
Makes 24 caps.

Sweet Sausage Stuffing

1 pound sweet Italian sausage, in bulk or four links, casings removed

1 package defrosted chopped frozen spinach, squeezed dry

1/2 stick butter, salted or unsalted

2 tablespoons extra-virgin olive oil

1/2 red bell pepper, seeded and finely diced

1/2 to 2/3 cup finely chopped mushroom stems (about 12 small stems or 2 to 3 portobello stems)

1 medium onion, chopped

2 cloves garlic, minced

A handful chopped fresh flat-leaf parsley

2 or 3 good pinches ground nutmeg

Black pepper, to taste

6 slices white bread, toasted and lightly buttered

1 egg

1/4 cup grated Parmigiano Reggiano cheese

Brown sausage in medium skillet over medium-high heat. Drain away fat. Transfer sausage to a bowl and combine with spinach. Wipe out pan and return to heat.

Melt butter and oil. Add peppers, mushrooms, onion, garlic, and parsley and cook until soft, 3 to 5 minutes, stirring frequently. Add sausage and spinach mixture to pan and combine. Sprinkle with nutmeg and pepper. Dice up toasted, buttered bread and add to pan. Scramble egg with cheese and pour over pan. Mush it all together to cook the egg. Stuff into pre-cooked mushroom caps and when ready to serve, brown under broiler. Makes enough stuffing for up to 24 large mushroom caps or 6 portobello caps.

Seafood Stuffing

1 stick butter, salted or unsalted
1 medium onion, chopped
2 cloves garlic, minced
2 stalks celery (from heart of stalk) finely chopped
1/2 red bell pepper, seeded and finely diced
A handful chopped fresh flat-leaf parsley
1 can (8 ounces) crab meat, drained
Coarse salt and black pepper, to taste
A couple pinches ground thyme
6 slices white bread, toasted and buttered
1 lemon

Melt butter in medium skillet over medium heat. Cook onion, garlic, celery, and bell pepper until soft, 8 to 10 minutes, stirring occasionally. Add parsley, crab meat, and seasonings. Combine well. Chop up toasted bread and add to pan. Squeeze the juice of one lemon over top of the pan. Mush it all up and stuff pre-cooked mushroom caps. Bake in 350° F oven for 10 minutes when you are ready to serve.

Hummus and Flat Breads

Hummus, the delicious blend of chick peas, garlic, and ground sesame, makes a great party dip. It is available, prepared and ready to serve, in many markets and in a variety of flavors. Buy 1 tub, a pound container, for every 6 guests. Transfer to a bowl and garnish with chopped parsley, scallions or crushed red pepper. Serve with a variety of flat breads and bread sticks, or celery sticks and scallions.

Cheese Board with Fresh and Dried Fruits, Smoked Almonds

Select up to four cheeses, about 1 1/2 to 2 pounds total, varying the colors and flavors from the specialty cheese case in your market. For a nice contrast, try green derby sage cheese, a red-tinted port-wine-veined derby and a smoked cheddar or Applewood smoked derby. Decorate with figs, dates, and dried pears. Serve with a dish of smokehouse almonds found in the snack and candy aisle in your market.

menu

Stuffed Portobellos

Giardiniera:
Marinated Carrot,
Cauliflower
and Pepper Salad

Antipasticks:
Skewered Italian Meats
and Cheeses

Fresh Figs and Melon
with Prosciutto

TIMING NOTE:
The marinated vegetables will take minutes to make, but
should be made at least one day before your party to allow
flavors to develop fully.

Stuffed Portobellos

4 tablespoons extra-virgin olive oil (four times around the pan)

6 portobello mushroom caps, stems removed (save 2 or 3 stems to chop for stuffing, if using sausage filling recipe)

4 cloves garlic, popped from skin

1/2 cup sherry, port or Marsala

Sausage or seafood stuffing, pages 172 and 173

1 package (10 ounces) shredded provolone or mozzarella cheese

Heat oil and garlic in a big skillet over medium heat. Cook mushroom tops until tender, 10 to 12 minutes, preparing stuffing while you wait. Douse pan with sherry, port or Marsala, coating caps. Remove caps from pan and place on cookie sheet. (Reserve juices in a small bowl and serve alongside stuffed mushrooms for dipping.)

Place a mound of sausage or seafood stuffing on half of each cap and top with a generous sprinkle of cheese. Fold the cap over, like an omelet. Place caps in 350° F oven for 5 minutes to melt cheese. Transfer to serving platter, cutting caps into pizza-like wedges and serve immediately. Makes 6 caps, enough for 12 servings.

Giardiniera

1 head cauliflower, stem removed and broken into florets

2 large carrots, peeled and thinly sliced

1/2 cup pepper rings, drained (found in Italian food aisle of market)

1/2 red bell pepper, seeded and chopped

Dressing:

1 cup white vinegar

1 teaspoon mustard seeds

1/2 teaspoon black peppercorns

1/4 cup sugar

Combine cauliflower, carrots, pepper rings, and bell pepper in bowl. Heat sugar, vinegar, mustard seeds, and peppercorns in a small saucepan over low heat until sugar dissolves. Pour marinade over veggies and refrigerate, stirring occasionally, for at least 24 hours. Drain and serve. Makes one quart of salad.

Antipasticks

1 pound provolone, cubed into 24 pieces (ask for 2, 1-inch thick hunks at deli)

2 dried Italian sausages, about 1 pound each (sopressata is the most common), cubed into 24 pieces — choose sweet or hot dried sausage, or mix Genoa or hard salamis cubed, as a substitute

Hot or sweet Italian cherry peppers

24 bamboo skewers (8-inch size)

Skewer ingredients, alternating 2 cubes of sausage or salami with 1 cube of cheese and one hot pepper to make each antipastick. Pile up on a platter and serve. Makes 24 skewers.

Fresh Figs and Melon with Prosciutto

8 fresh figs, sliced

1 ripe cantaloupe, sliced

1/2 pound thinly sliced proscuitto di Parma (available at deli counter)

Arrange figs and cantaloupe on a serving platter with thinly sliced prosciutto, for an elegant Italian offering. Makes 12 servings.

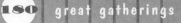
menu

Emmanuel's Caponata: Eggplant, Pepper, and Tomato Appetizer

Dried Sausages, Olive, and Cheese Board

White Bean Dip and Garlic Toasts

TIMING NOTES:
While caponata cooks, put together cheese and sausage board and prepare dip.

Emmanuel Nini's Caponata (Party Version)

3 cloves garlic, minced

1/4 teaspoon crushed red pepper, a pinch or two

3 tablespoons extra-virgin olive oil (two or three times around the pan)

1 red bell pepper, chopped

1 green bell pepper, chopped

1 medium Spanish onion, chopped

1 medium eggplant, chopped

3 stalks celery from the heart, chopped

1/4 pound green and black olives, pitted

1 palmful golden raisins (about 1/4 cup packed)

3 tablespoons, a palmful, capers

Kosher salt, to taste

1 can (28 ounces) diced tomatoes

1 can (13 ounces) crushed tomatoes

A handful chopped fresh flat-leaf parsley

1 round loaf crusty Italian bread, top cut off and insides scooped out (save the top)

1 bottle (3 ounces) pine nuts/pignoli, toasted in oven until golden brown

In a deep skillet or pot, working over medium heat, simmer garlic and crushed pepper in oil until the garlic speaks. Add peppers, onion, eggplant, celery, olives, raisins, capers, and Kosher salt. Cover pan and cook the vegetables down, stirring occasionally, until eggplant begins to breakdown, about 10 to 12 minutes.

Add tomatoes and parsley. Heat through and cook until all vegetables are tender. Turn off heat. Dump caponata into bread bowl. Place bread in center of platter. Cut top of bread into cubes and surround bowl with the cubes for dipping. Sprinkle caponata with toasted nuts. Serves 8 to 12, as a party offering.

White Bean Dip and Garlic Toasts

Toasts:
2 baguettes, sliced at the bakery counter in market
1/2 cup extra-virgin olive oil
2 cloves garlic, popped from skin

Dip:
2 cans (15 ounces each) white cannellini beans, drained
1/3 cup extra-virgin olive oil
2 cloves garlic, popped from skin
Coarse salt and black pepper, to taste
4 sprigs fresh rosemary, leaves stripped from stem

Heat oven to 325° F. Place sliced baguettes on cookie sheets in a single layer. Toast for 10 minutes or until lightly golden. Heat oil and garlic in ovensafe dish in microwave for 45 seconds on high. Brush toasts with a dab of garlic oil and place in a basket to serve alongside dip.

Place beans in food processor. Heat 1/3 cup oil and garlic in microwave on high for 45 seconds. Add oil, garlic, salt, pepper, and rosemary to beans. Process dip until smooth and transfer to a serving dish.

Dried Sausages Olives and Cheese Board

Arrange dried sausages, like sopressata, available at the deli in your market, with two or three selections of Italian cheeses, from the specialty cheese case, on a cutting board. Allow 2 pounds of cheeses and 2 pounds of meat, total, for 12 guests.

Decorate board with mixed olives from the bulk section of deli. One pound will be more than enough. Place olives in small piles on beds of pretty lettuce leaves or in small glass bowls. When board is arranged, combine your dip in a food processor.

menu

**Pot Sticker Pockets:
Pork and Vegetable-Filled
Hors d'oeuvres**

**Exotic Fruit and
Cheese Board**

Fried Noodles and Duck Sauce

**Fortune Cookies,
Candied Nuts, and Ginger**

Pot Sticker Pockets
(Party Version)

1 1/2 pounds ground pork

1/2 cup (a good handful) chopped water chestnuts

2 green onions, chopped

2 tablespoons soy sauce (several good shakes)

1/2 teaspoon ground ginger or 1-inch piece fresh gingerroot, grated

2 cloves garlic, minced

A pinch crushed red pepper

1/2 orange (grate the outer skin into bowl, then juice the orange into mixture)

8 large 9- to 12-inch flour tortilla wraps

Topping:

2 teaspoons honey

1/4 cup white vinegar

1 cucumber, seeded, peeled, thinly sliced

1/2 carrot shredded

Hoisin sauce (available on the Asian foods aisle of the market)
Bibb lettuce leaves, shredded

> "These finger sandwich pockets taste like a giant Chinese dumpling."

Combine pork and next 7 ingredients in a bowl. Form into patties and cook for 5 minutes on each side in grill pan or nonstick skillet over medium-high heat.

Mix honey and vinegar and coat cucumber and carrot in the dressing. Wash and dry one head bibb lettuce leaves. Shred by thinly slicing. Warm tortilla according to package directions.

To assemble, brush tortilla with hoisin sauce. Place a palmful of lettuce in center of tortilla. Top with a couple of scoops of shredded carrot and cucumber mixture, and 1 pork pattie. Wrap tortilla up and over on all 4 sides and flip entire square-shaped packet over. Cut in half from corner to corner, then half again, forming four triangle-shaped pockets. Place a toothpick through the center of each triangle to make them easier for your guests to pick up. Makes 36 triangles.

Exotic Fruit and Cheese Board

1/2 pound each, 4 assorted soft and hard cheeses (found in the specialty cheese case of your market)

Tangerines

Fresh figs

Other tropical fruits, sliced

Arrange the cheese on a cutting board with tangerine sections, figs, and other tropical fruits of your choice.

Fried Noodles and Duck Sauce

These popular fried noodles are the kind you get as munchies in Chinese restaurants. They are packaged and found in the Asian food aisle of your market.

Duck sauce makes a great dip.

Fortune Cookies, Candied Nuts, and Ginger

Look for fortune cookies, too, in the Asian food aisle of your market. Candied nuts can often be found in the bulk foods section of your market, while candied ginger is usually stocked in the spice or baking aisle.

Not Your Mamma's Meatballs

**fabulous recipes**

Chinese Checkers:
Spicy Chicken Balls

The Gingerbread Man's
Meatballs:
Gingered Meatballs

Spicy Beef Balls

Curry Beef Balls

Minted Meat Balls

Chinese Checkers: Spicy Chicken Balls

1 1/2 pounds ground chicken

3 tablespoons (several shakes) soy sauce

2 pinches ground ginger

A pinch cayenne pepper

2 cloves garlic, minced

Black pepper, to taste

A handful chopped cilantro or parsley

1 cored fresh pineapple, drained and cubed (found in produce departments)

2 tablespoons sesame or peanut oil

Hoisin sauce (a barbecue-style sauce found in Asian foods aisle)

Bamboo skewers or toothpicks

Mix chicken with soy sauce, ginger, cayenne, garlic, pepper, and cilantro or parsley. Form into 20 balls. Heat oil in skillet over medium high heat. Cook balls for 6 minutes, giving the pan several shakes as they cook. Cut one open to make sure chicken is cooked through. Add pineapple chunks and remove from heat. Drop 3 or 4 serving-size spoonfuls of hoisin into pan and shake to coat the balls and pineapple. Transfer to serving dish and serve with bamboo skewers or toothpicks. Serves 8 to 12 as party food.

The Gingerbread Man's Meatballs: Gingered Meatballs

1 1/2 pounds ground beef
1 cup crushed ginger snaps (use your food processor to crumb them)
1/2 cup bread crumbs
1 egg or equivalent egg substitute
1/2 medium onion, minced
1 teaspoon allspice
1 tablespoon ground cumin
1/2 teaspoon ground ginger or 1 tablespoon grated fresh
Ground black pepper and salt, to taste
1 tablespoon extra-virgin olive oil (once around the pan)
1 tablespoon butter
1 can (14 ounces) no-fat, reduced-salt beef broth
1 lemon
2 to 3 tablespoons brown sugar (a handful)
A handful chopped fresh flat-leaf parsley

Combine beef, 1/2 cup of the ginger snap crumbs, bread crumbs, egg, onion, spices, and salt and pepper in a bowl. Do not over mix. Form into 2-inch balls.

Heat oil and butter over medium high-heat. Brown meatballs evenly, about 5 minutes. Add broth, the juice of 1 lemon, brown sugar and the remaining 1/2 cup ginger snap crumbs to the pan. Cook until the cookie crumbs dissolve into the sauce, stirring carefully and frequently. Stir in parsley. Drop heat down a bit and cover and cook another 10 minutes.

Dump into serving dish and serve with bamboo skewers for picking. Serves 10 to 12 as party offering.

Spicy Beef Balls

1 1/2 pounds ground beef

2 cloves garlic, minced

1 egg

1 tablespoon plus one teaspoon Dijon mustard

1 handful capers, cracked with the flat of your knife

1/2 cup Italian bread crumbs

A handful chopped fresh flat-leaf parsley

1 lemon

Cracked black pepper and Kosher salt, to taste

6 shakes Worcestershire sauce

2 tablespoons extra-virgin olive oil (twice around the pan)

1 can (14 ounces) reduced-salt beef broth

Combine beef, garlic, egg, the teaspoon of Dijon, capers, bread crumbs, parsley, juice of only 1/2 of the lemon, and salt and pepper. Form 2-inch balls. Heat oil in skillet over medium-high heat. Brown balls for 5 minutes. Add broth, tablespoon of Dijon and juice of the remaining half lemon. Cook for additional 10 minutes. Transfer to a serving dish and serve with bamboo skewers for picking. Feeds 10 to 12 as a party fare.

Curry Beef Balls

1 1/2 pounds ground beef

1 medium onion, chopped

Half a palmful curry powder, about 1 rounded tablespoon

6 drops Worcestershire

1 egg

1/2 cup bread crumbs

2/3 cup mincemeat (found in baking aisle of the market)

Salt, to taste

A pinch or two cayenne pepper

1 tablespoon sesame oil (found in Asian foods aisle)

2 scallions, thinly sliced

2 tablespoons sesame seeds

Preheat oven to 425° F.

Combine beef, onion, curry powder, Worcestershire, egg, bread crumbs, mince-meat, salt, cayenne, and sesame oil in a bowl. Roll 1-inch balls and place on nonstick cookie sheet. Bake 10 to 12 minutes or until balls are evenly browned. Remove from oven and transfer to serving dish. Sprinkle with scallions and sesame seeds. Serve with bamboo skewers for picking. Serves 10 to 12 as party fare.

Minted Meat Balls

1 1/2 pounds ground beef or 1 pound ground beef combined with 1/2 pound ground lamb

1 egg

3 cloves garlic, minced

1/2 cup bread crumbs

4 sprigs fresh mint leaves, chopped

1/2 lemon

6 drops Worcestershire sauce

Coarse salt and black pepper, to taste

2 scallions, thinly sliced

Dipping sauce:

1 cup plain yogurt

1/2 cup mint jelly

2 sprigs fresh thyme

Preheat oven to 425° F.

Combine beef, or beef and lamb, with egg, garlic, bread crumbs, mint, the juice of 1/2 lemon, Worcestershire, and salt and pepper. Roll into 1 1/2-inch balls and place on a nonstick cookie sheet. Bake for 10 to 12 minutes, until browned. Blend yogurt, jelly and thyme in processor or blender. Transfer meatballs to serving dish with dip in smaller dish placed at the center. Serves 10 to 12 as party food.